The Young Woman's Guide
TO LIBERATION

KAREN DeCROW

The Young

Woman's Guide to

LIBERATION

Alternatives to a Half-Life

While the Choice Is Still Yours

PEGASUS

A DIVISION OF THE BOBBS-MERRILL
COMPANY, INCORPORATED, PUBLISHERS
INDIANAPOLIS · NEW YORK

Copyright © 1971 by The Bobbs-Merrill Company, Inc.
Printed in the United States of America.
Library of Congress Catalog Card Number: 72-141377
ISBN 0-672-63615-8 (pbk)
ISBN 0-672-53615-3
Second Printing

To my mother,
Juliette Abt Lipschultz,
with love

Acknowledgments

I would like to thank the following people, each of whom helped me in the preparation of this book: Nola Claire, Roger DeCrow, Marguerite J. Fisher, Julian Franklin, Paula Franklin, Betty Friedan, J. William Hicks, Jacqueline Reinach, Betty Bone Schiess, Faith Seidenberg, Robert Seidenberg, and Nancy G. Thomas.

Particular thanks is in order to the following people, who read parts of my manuscript, making helpful suggestions: Janice D'Amico, Claudia Lipschultz, Amie Mohr, Irene Pardee, Lisa Seidenberg, Jeanne Valentino, and Lynn Woodcock.

Contents

Disturb the universe?

The Seventh Wave

For her world is her husband, her family, her children and her home. . . . We do not find it right when the woman presses into the world of the man. . . . The man upholds the nation as the woman upholds the family. . . . Reason is dominant in man. He searches, analyses and often opens new immeasurable realms.

Adolf Hitler, 1934

If you had an investment in a bank you wouldn't want the president of your bank making a loan under these raging hormonal influences at that particular [menstrual] period. . . . It would be safer to entrust a male pilot's reactions and judgments in a difficult in-flight or landing problem than to even a slightly pregnant female pilot.

Dr. Edgar F. Berman, former member of the Democratic Party's National Priorities Committee, August 1970.

Jack and Jill went up the hill
To fetch a pail of water.
Jack fell down and broke his crown,
And Jill came tumbling after.

Do I dare
Disturb the universe?

T. S. Eliot, *The Love Song of J. Alfred Prufrock*

The other day a bright, attractive woman in her forties described to a social group how she had skillfully conquered a business situation in her personal life. I complimented her: "You should be a lawyer." Her reply was: "I would rather be a girl."

Hearing that comment is credentials enough to write this book. But I have others. I came of age in the 50's at the height of the feminine mystique; I am a member of a family which believes that winning a husband beats winning the Nobel Prize; I attended schools where bright women are all nervously trying to keep their mouths shut; although a victim of myopia-near-blindness, I was counseled never to wear my glasses when "a male was present," and once stepped gracefully into a car not my date's because I could not see a thing; I have worked for ten years, always for men who are earning three-to-ten times what I am, and who are often not outstanding; I am married.

However, my main qualification for writing a book on the big brainwash is that I am a woman.

Growing up female in America today, one gets a very clear message: it is basically the same from our parents, from our teachers, from our religious advisers, from our psychiatrists, from the mass media. It very quickly becomes what we tell ourselves. The message is simple. As Simone deBeauvoir expressed it, men are punished for being failures, women are punished for being successes.

The makers of Barbie doll express it in their ads. The Mattel Company makes a game, The World of Space, "because boys have always landed on the moon." It makes the Tog'l game "because boys were born to build and learn." It makes the Super-Eyes telescope "because boys are curious about things big and small." It makes the Injector game "because he'd like to operate his own factory." It makes toys for "girls who love pretty things."

And "because wishing you were older is part of growing up, Mattel makes The World of Barbie. Here's the best scene around. Barbie and her friends doing the in things girls should do. And Barbie and her crowd talk about it too! Talk about new places to visit, new clothes to wear."

In 1837, women realized that it was not only the (black) slaves who needed to be liberated. The women who formally launched the women's rights movement at Seneca Falls, New York, met each other when they were refused seats at an anti-slavery convention in London. Shut off behind a curtain in the gallery, Elizabeth Cady Stanton, on her honeymoon, and Lucretia Mott, mother of five, decided to take things into their own hands, to fight for themselves.

"A great idea in the background of dim consciousness is like a phantom ocean beating upon the shores of human life in successive waves of specialization. A whole succession of such waves are as dreams slowly doing their work of sapping the base of some cliff or habit: but the seventh wave is a revolution—and the nations echo round."[1]

Why we in 1970 are still a second-class caste is a long story; but the "seventh wave is a revolution," and the women's movement today is indeed that seventh wave.

Women are helpmates, in the house and out of it. We make pottery instead of becoming professional artists. We join the League of Women Voters instead of entering political life. We raise money for the symphony instead of playing first violin. When the male leaves adolescence, he concludes his search for the better hair cream and the sexier girl, and goes on to better things. We women have no such luck. And since no one, male or female, can derive ultimate gratification simply from pleasing a member of the opposite sex, the young girl is doomed, from birth, to disappointment.

American women, however, keep trying. 59% of all women go to the beauty parlor at least once a week[2], no doubt harboring the view that they need perfect hair to attract and/or keep their man. Even then, however, they still feel unsure.

A friend, a Phi Beta Kappa, wrote me:

> I feel the same need to do something worthwhile myself. Is this just a sympton of middle age, of taking stock of what we live for? Our families, of course, but the older boys are busy with their own interests. X, who is twelve, and Y, who is nine, still need me of course. But many of the occupations which kept me busy with the older ones —PTA, dancing school, scouting, etc., I've simply eliminated and I'm sure they aren't really important at all. I believe I've become very cynical about women's organizations and much of their "busywork."

Miriam Ringo, a management consultant, recently completed "The Well-Placed Wife," a study of women married to top Chicago-area business and professional men. When respondents were asked, "If you could lead your adult life over again, what would you do?" most answered they would get a more career-oriented education and pursue a career.

A further example of housewife discontent comes to us from Japan.[3] "Of nineteen call girls recently arrested and charged with prostitution, twelve turned out to be housewives in their early thirties with children under ten. Asked to explain their wayward behavior, the wives said they were tired of staying at home, they wanted extra pocket money, their husbands could not provide them with sexual satisfaction. Among the wives arrested were those of several high government officials and a leading Japanese publisher."

The complaints of women are partially encompassed by saying wives are bored, don't have enough money, and don't get enough sex in the monogamous situation. But a further complaint is that we are all aware, consciously or otherwise, of the misogyny in the men we live with. In the armed services, for example, a recruit training group which fails to perform is called a "bunch of women" by the instructor.

Since men define our mental health, their own misogyny cannot fail to pervade our own notions of ourselves. Babies are raised by the words of Spock, Gesell, Ginott, and Bettelheim (all men). These men learned their theory from Freud, Adler, and Fromm (all men). The doctors themselves often realize the male chauvinist trap they are helping to construct:

> In trying to bring about change, women unfortunately will not be able to count on much support from the psycho-analysts. For, as we have seen, the preconceptions of psychoanalysis about the proper feminine role prevent them from really helping a girl successfully to grow up female —that is, to become female in the sexual relations and in child-rearing, and yet to develop fully as a male does in all other respects.[4]

Even the "sex" doctors have traditional views on sex roles. Dr. David Reuben, author of the best-selling *Everything You Always Wanted to Know About Sex—But Were Afraid to Ask*, has dispelled many myths about sexuality. However, he is true to form, in having a "slave" in his home.[5] "Reuben's wife, who, when in New York, devotedly stays in the Plaza Hotel washing his shirts, says the doctor solves his own problems by 'eliminating all the emotion and seeing it as it is. Then with a smile that seems frozen . . . she adds that her husband did not force her to type the book. 'But he didn't want to deny me the privilege.' "

I may be wrong, but I venture the guess that hundreds of thousands of women have typed manuscripts for their lovers and husbands, and that the number of males who have provided similar service for the women in their lives can be counted on the fingers of one hand.

Mrs. Reuben, according to the American way of life, is reaping social esteem by ironing the shirts of a best-selling author. In Scandinavia, where life is more civilized, she would not get points for this. Kaare Svalastoga, the Danish sociologist, reports that even if a Scandinavian woman excels in being a good housekeeper and hostess, a loving mother, and an attractive spouse, she will reap slight social esteem because dominant middle-class opinion will insist on the superior value of choosing a career outside the home and of cultivating literary and artistic interests. "Few Swedish wives give up careers when they marry; few American wives have careers to give up."[6]

It would be misleading, however, to say that distrust and hatred of the female is unique to the United States. One fascinating avenue for examining misogyny is to look at menstrual taboos throughout the world. What better way to establish caste than to find some unalterable physical characteristic (black skin, a monthly period) and then assign status in life on the basis of it.

H. R. Hays, in *The Dangerous Sex: The Myth of Feminine Evil*,[7] reports on menstrual taboos throughout the world:

> Siberian Samoyed women step over fires of burning reindeer skin. They must also refrain from cooking food for their men. Among the Nootka of the Canadian northwest coast, at her first period a girl is given her private eating utensils and must eat alone for eight months. The Chippewa girl also eats alone, cannot cross a public road or talk to any man or boy. Eskimo girls at their first period are taboo for forty days. They must sit crouching in a corner, their faces to the wall, draw their hoods over their heads, let their hair hang over their faces and only leave the house when everyone else is asleep. Hermann Ploss described a still more curious segregation practiced by the Australians of Queensland. The girl is taken to a shady place. Her mother draws a circle on the ground and

digs a deep hole into which the girl must step. The sandy soil is then filled in, leaving her buried up to the waist. A woven hedge of branches or twigs is set around her with an opening toward which she turns her face. Her mother kindles a fire at the opening, the girl remains in her nest of earth in a squatting posture with folded arms and hands resting downward on the sand heap that covers her lower limbs. . . . The Hindus observed an endless number of prohibitions during the first three days of a woman's period. She must not weep, mount a horse, an ox, or an elephant, be carried in a palanquin or drive in a vehicle. In Hebrew tradition the menstruating woman is forbidden to work in a kitchen, sit at meals with other people, or drink from a glass used by others. Any contact with her husband is a sin and the penalty for intercourse during her period is death for both. Indeed the misfortunes which men suffer when they break the menstrual taboo vary but they are always severe. A Uganda Bantu woman by touching her husband's effects makes him sick; if she lays a hand on his weapons, he will be killed in the next fight. The natives of Malacca believe that coitus, or even contact, will cause the man to lose his virility.

. . . the male attitude toward female sexual functions is basically apprehensive; women, in short, are dangerous. Taboos and fears of contagion, however, are not limited to the physical crises in their lives. When we investigate the ideas of contact still further, a host of activities requires avoidance of women in general.

Dr. Hayes points out that in most cultures we are "dangerous." I would go a step further and say that we are *unclean*, to be avoided as food handlers during menstruation. This extends very conveniently to participation in the society in general, whether we menstruate or not. Orthodox Jewish women, for example, cannot say the most holy prayers, because they "might be menstruating."

No girl, forced to sit waist-high in sand, could possibly interpret that entering womanhood is an event of joy. And, any woman who observes men closely, cannot help but notice their aversion to women: be it our menstrual periods or the idea of a woman as President of the United States.

What then are we good for? One thing is keeping the products moving. Betty Friedan pointed out in *The Feminine Mystique* that Madison Avenue could not possibly unload a new refrigerator every two years on the American family unless the wife was bored and listless enough to think that a revamped kitchen could revamp her life. National Beauty Queen Week is "to call local and national attention to the promotion of beauty queens and their value to the economy."[8]

We are used as a means of moving the merchandise. And the top executives of the companies which manufacture the merchandise are men, the heads of the advertising agencies that push the merchandise are men. The mass media are in the hands of men: they write the scripts, they produce the shows, for male heads of advertising agencies and sponsors. The magazine which says "Never underestimate the power of a woman"—the *Ladies Home Journal*—apparently does just that. The three top editorial positions are held by men. *Good Housekeeping* has a woman in the fourth editorial position; the top three editors are men. Elizabeth Pope Frank (number 4) does not think too highly of her sisters, the readers. "Almost any national issue can be put in terms women can understand . . . pollution is one example of the kind of issues that can be translated into words that mean something to the everyday woman," she told the *Miami Herald*.[9] "During the 40's I don't think *Good Housekeeping* ever referred to the war. . . . We don't think women's magazines should be too heavily weighted down with social issues."

The women's magazines do not cater to women's minds; the pornography does not cater to our bodies. Stanley Kauffman writes in the *New Republic*[10] that it must be recognized that pornography is meant for men, not women. This can be proved by the simple fact that women are paid more for the participation in pornographic films; men will often do them for nothing.

The movies, since the 30s when a film heroine could be a career woman and get away with it, have consistently showed that we willingly give up all ego-gratification for "love." A typical film of the 40s, *Take a Letter, Darling*, has Rosalind Russell, a female executive, hiring Fred MacMurray as her secretary. He is mocked by everyone in the office, and finally she falls in love with him and gives up her job. In the films of the 60s, women are rarely executives even at the start of the story. We please our men by being domestic. In *The Fortune Cookie*, for example, an ex-wife who wants to show her husband she is going to be "good," makes an energetic display of cooking gourmet food, vacuuming the floor, cleaning the apartment.

The networks are very honest about their sexism. CBS ran the following ad: "We've got something she wants—diversion. Forty-one million women like her spend ten hours a week watching daytime TV. And she's got something we want, buying power. When she's not using the soaps, detergents, powders and polishes, she watches TV to learn about the soap, detergents, powders and polishes that she is going to buy."[11]

The idiocy, the danger, of the idea that human needs can be met by a product of course affects men as well as women. But the ads consistently show an anti-female bias. We need men to explain the intricacies of using the new soap powder. Franchellie Cadwell, a New York advertising woman, said "The rationale behind most of the demeaning commercials is that male-dominated ad agencies think the nation's 66 million housewives are possessed by infantile fantasies and a cleanliness neurosis."[12]

We require constant coaching by men on how to do our floors, our dishes, our woodwork, our wash.

TV commercials once in a great while permit the housewife to get out of the kitchen. She gets to go to the laundromat. Here, we can vie with envy for the whitest wash, hating with a passion any fellow woman who doesn't have ring around her husband's collar. Ajax: "I need all the cleaning power I can get. Have you ever seen a whiter white?" Cold Power: "It was turning my husband's underwear pink that got me into hot water."

Many commercials do not just show us as moronic, but are outright antagonistic to us. Deserta gelatin advertises: Fat girls have more time for a business career than others. A suitcase is run over by a dopey wife who cannot see where she is driving. It doesn't crush. (This, despite the fact that women are better, safer drivers; have lower insurance rates.) A new series of products, to eliminate "female odor," have replaced the former products which eliminated dog odor. The best cigarettes are like the best women—thin and rich. And of course, the famous "You've come a long way baby." All the way to our own cigarette.

Teenage magazines are junior copies of what Mommy reads. *Seventeen*, for example, concentrates on fashion, home and food, with a secondary but heavy emphasis on love, marriage, and dating. "Are you madly in love, gladly in love—or is that special person still to be found?"[13]

Preparation for living in the suburbs is given many pages. Table settings: silverware, china, and glassware are supposed to appeal to the teenage girl. Keeping women in the home is part of a long-time tradition of women's magazines. A PhD dissertation by Esta Klein Seaton[14] documented that the *Journal* from the period 1890–1919, looked with disfavor on all activities that took women out of the home. The magazine's most ambitious at-

tempt to resolve the dilemma of women's being gain-
fully employed was the development of the formula of
the helpful wife and efficient housewife, a formulation
that gave to housekeeping the status of a profession and
credited the businesslike housewife with directly contributing to her husband's earning capacity. However, the
magazine was not fully able to resolve the contradiction
between its idealization of the passive, innocent, dependent woman whose interests were entirely home-
centered and its simultaneous approval of the efficient,
intelligent, active woman.

Life Magazine had this to say about the women's revolution on January 29, 1945: "Of all the social revolutions
now abroad in the world, that of the American woman
is the least dynamic, the least predictable, the most aim-
less and divided—in short the most feminine."

The over 6,500,000 readers of *Glamour* are, twenty-five
years later, still helplessly "feminine": "Help! make me a
beauty. Help! my skin tone is a drag. Help! My hair is
a nothing color. Help! My eyes are a real loss. Help!
Make me over, and do it NOW."[15]

Cosmopolitan has sprung us all the way from the kitchen
to the bedroom. The Cosmopolitan girl learned this summer twenty-three ways to kiss. *Vogue*, which appears to
keep us safely out of the kitchen, still praises the feminine mystique. It featured an article,[16] by a male gyne-
cologist, on how to keep the body fit (in order, presumably, to wear all the pretty, expensive *Vogue* fashions).
He wrote:

> Physiologically, the ideal life for a woman would be
> that of some primitive societies where a women's life from
> age 14, or younger, is a continuous cycle of pregnancy,
> lactation, and conception. . . . One aspect of primitive life
> life that today's young women are adopting enthusiastically
> is natural childbirth. They love it. And so do their obste-
> tricians. Natural childbirth is the normal thing. Young

people now want close relationships, they want the husband in the delivery room, the baby with them afterwards. There is an increasing demand for rooming-in wards. They want to feed the baby themselves.

The political implications of being pregnant all the time are apparent: one cannot achieve much in the outer world if life is a continuous round of visits to the maternity ward. Since this doctor is writing for *Vogue*, he wants to assure his readers that their beauty will not be affected by steady pregnancies, or by intercourse. "Will breast feeding cause sagging of the breast later on? No . . . We now know that the breast goes through intense activity during sexual intercourse. Changes occur in size, shape; blood flow is increased. All this helps to maintain it."

In the magazine fiction of today, the career women seldom appears. One recent study[17] showed that only 4% of the fictional females in women's magazines have careers, and only 7% of the fictional marriages are unhappy.

Women's magazines continue to devote many of their articles to wives of famous men. *McCall's* is planning a piece on the wife of Supreme Court Justice Harry A. Blackmun, focusing on her fondness for home sewing.

Readers of women's magazines are told in clinical detail how other women behave sexually. Yet physical love is conspicuously absent from all the magazines' fiction. The *Ladies Home Journal* removed all the "dirty" language and most of the sex when it excerpted Jacqueline Susann's *The Love Machine*. In Erich Segal's novel *Love Story*, a young girl tells her husband, "Get your ass home to my dinner table." The *Ladies Home Journal* changed this to, "Zoom on home to my dinner table."[18]

The mass press in general considers it "her" dinner table, and didn't, for many years, want to deal with the idea that women belonged any place but serving dinner. Several years ago, *The Saturday Evening Post* asked Caroline Bird to investigate sex discrimination and write an article about it. She told them that women were not discriminated against, but that she would do the story anyway. As she did her research, she found such gross sex discrimination that the *Post* would not publish her report. The result was that she wrote the excellent book, *Born Female: The High Cost of Keeping Women Down*. Miss Bird told the Associated Press (May 20, 1970): "And the rage which prompted me to do it is in every woman, even in those who say they don't want equality and who say they don't want to be bothered by all the fuss. In their case, it's a matter of 'The lady doth protest too much.'"

To me, the magazine image of the smiling mother making a souffle is the same as the magazine image of the nude "bunny," reclining on a fur rug. Each relegates us to the role of object—be it kitchen object or sex object. Each shows us as important because we *please men*—be it via the stomach or another part of the anatomy.

The *Playboy* philosophy, however, deserves some mention of its own. It is particularly dangerous because it pretends to liberate women, using some childlike intellectualization that being free in bed is being free. Hugh Hefner apparently considers women's liberation a danger to his profits. In Chicago, Shelley Schlicker was fired by *Playboy* for revealing an internal policy memorandum about the women's liberation movement to other employees of *Playboy*. The memo, from Hugh Hefner to an editor, called for a "devastating" and "non-objective" article on women's liberation for the May 1970 issue; it identified the women's liberation movement as "the natural enemy." Apparently, an article had been written for *Playboy* on women's lib, and never published, because it depicted the movement as a good thing. In the article finally published, the women's revolution was shown to be fought by lesbians, neurotics, and "very unnatural" women. It is reassuring to know that the *Playboy* enterprise, which makes millions of dollars on our bodies, is beginning to be nervous.

Far from altering his policy to fit the new temper of the women's movement, Hefner has made a fresh investment in women-as-objects. The *Stewardess and Flight Service News* reports[19] that

> A new horizon has opened up for the stewardess profession. It's now possible to be a Jet Bunny on Hugh Herner's "Big Bunny," a 38-passenger DC-9. . . . Jet Bunnies must be first and foremost Playboy Bunnies. The new Jet Bunnies were chosen from more than 800 Bunnies in Playboy Clubs and Playboy Club-Hotels in the United States and abroad and were trained by Continental Airlines, with Purdue Airlines giving them their post-graduate course in how to operate the specialized equipment aboard the Big Bunny. Part of the Bunnies' training at Continental included learning to prepare the elaborate gourmet meals planning for the Big Bunny. . . . The rear section of the Big Bunny contains Hefner's private quarters, which have a separate entrance. The compartment has a large 6' by 8' elliptical bed. . . . A unique shower has also been installed for Hefner. The special compartment is fitted with two decorative shower heads, fed from a 30-gallon water tank.

Elizabeth Fisher, editor of *Aphra* (named to honor Aphra Behn, the seventeenth-century woman who is said to be the first professional writer of her sex), started this first feminist literary magazine because the existing journals would not publish material showing women as full-functioning adults. "There is a certain strain in the writings of women that male editors just won't touch. If a woman is depicted as evil and destructive, that's all right; but if she is a nice person, just strong and rebellious, they feel threatened."[20]

Hefner won't publish a study of women's liberation

which shows the women involved to be intelligent and healthy; *The Saturday Evening Post* commissions an article on sex discrimination and, when the author finds out the enormous extent to which it exists, won't publish it; the so-called intellectuals share the same male supremacist bias.

Changing the role of women, apparently, is the most revolutionary kind of restructuring of human society. Male protest echoes from all quarters: hard-hat, playboy, intellectual. What we are saying is that sex differences are great fun in bed. But every place else they serve to keep women down, to deny us full participation in the world.

The women of today are more ambitious: we want as much pleasure out in the city as we have been granted in the bedroom.

NOTES TO INTRODUCTION

1. Alfred North Whitehead.
2. *New York Times*, July 15, 1970.
3. *Parade* Magazine, June 21, 1970.
4. Dr. Bruno Bettelheim, in "Growing Up Female," *Harper's*, October 1962.
5. *Look*, July 14, 1970.
6. Kaare Svalastoga.
7. H. R. Hays, in *The Dangerous Sex: The Myth of Feminine Evil*. New York: G. P. Putnam's Sons, 1964, pp. 40–44.
8. *Time*, August 10, 1970.
9. *Miami Herald*, April 23, 1970.
10. *New Republic*, July 1970.
11. *New York Times*, January 5, 1970.
12. *Syracuse Herald-Journal*, June 16, 1970.
13. *Seventeen*, June 1970.
14. Esta Klein Seaton, "The Changing Image of the American Woman in a Mass-Circulation Periodical: *The Ladies Home Journal, 1890–1919*."
15. *Glamour*, July 1970.
16. *Vogue*, February 1970.
17. *The Wall Street Journal*, August 3, 1970.
18. Reported in *The Wall Street Journal*, August 3, 1970.
19. *Stewardess and Flight Service News*, May 1970.
20. Elizabeth Fisher, reported in *New York Times*, August 1970.

The Young Woman's Guide
TO LIBERATION

and her husband, of course...
spends her time writing, lecturing, and traveling, counsels
women to stay at home. She says women are happier

CHAPTER I

Sisterhood and Self-Love: 6,000 Years of Vying for the King's Approval

*T*HERE IS no question that one of the major reasons that women have not been able to raise our status in the world, during thousands of years of exploitation, is that we have very few feelings of sisterhood, and practically no self-love. Women do hate women; women do think men are superior.

The lack of self-confidence in women has three explanations. The first is that men, who run everything, say women are inferior. The second is that the few women who have made it in the world often say that they are special, and that other women belong in the home. The movement, of course, has changed this, but the woman growing up in America up until a few years ago never received encouragement from her successful sisters.

Ann Landers, who writes a nationally syndicated column, and has hundreds of people working for her, while she spends her time writing, lecturing, and traveling, counsels women to stay at home. She says women are happier there. Phylis McGinley, a world renowned poet, who has a similarly exciting, vital life—writes poems about the joys of the kitchen and the nursery. I have been interviewed by several prominent women television personalities, who, although they spend their time in a public job, say loud and clear that women should be wives and mothers. Cher, of Sonny and Cher, who by her own statements, does not cook or clean and has maids to take care of her child, doesn't believe in women's liberation, because its tenets go "against woman's nature."

The third reason why women do not love themselves and other women is that we see a certain reality. Since in our society women *do not* hold positions of power, any girl with half a brain quickly realizes that the only way she can get to power is through a man. She must marry him, or at least be his lover. She may succeed by working for him. Because women cannot earn much money on their own, because hardly any women hold political office, women quickly get the message that gaining success by currying favor with the male is not some silly plot concocted by one's mother or by the women's magazines: it is true. So, women then embark on the self-defeating road of competing *against each other* for the favor and affections of the male. This competition keeps us effectively out of the competition for success in the world; we are too busy working against each other.

As John Stuart Mill said,[1] women have no choice but to identify with the oppressor. What is in it for them if they don't? We women observe that none of our kind occupy positions of power or interest in the society, and of course we conclude that we are all inferior.

When Gallup asked both men and women whether they would vote for a woman for President of the United States, 45% of the men, but only 25% of the women, said "yes." Given the roles that most women play in this country today, this is not surprising. When you spend your days in the home, even acknowledging that one like you could run the country would be an unnerving idea. It would cast some doubt on your own *raison d'être*.

So, we compete with other women for the favor of the King—the best man around. The smartest, the richest, the best looking, the most athletic. And one cannot help the competition, other women.

The ten most admired women in America, last year, were eight wives (Mrs. Dwight Eisenhower, Mrs. Robert Kennedy, etc.) and two movie stars.

Women who are out in the world are still apologizing to themselves, and to the men around them. Stanlee Miller Coy, author of *The Single Girl's Book: Making It in the Big City*[2] ends her Acknowledgments:

> Finally, the greatest debt is owed to my husband, Wayne, who read and reread the manuscript, making helpful suggestions, who suffered without complaint hasty meals and casual housekeeping, and who never suggested that his wife might be better organized in her work and *less obsessed by it* (italics mine) since this was, after all, their first year of marriage.

Ms. Coy's book, which gives much good practical advice, but which perpetuates the myth that being single is a curse, also keeps women in their place in other, more subtle ways. In the chapter on "Choosing a Doctor," she uses the exclusive pronoun "he." Although (only) 7% of the doctors in the United States are women (the lowest percentage of women in the profession in any Western country), they are invisible to the author, another woman.

The medical profession does much to relegate us to our biological functions, to our selfless nonindividualistic identity. Instead of a pregnancy's being treated as something which can go on concidentally with other life activities, the pregnant woman in America is encouraged to coddle herself, before and after childbirth. This may be payment, in part, for relegating her to biological functions in the first place.

Gynecologists and obstetricians typically have an attitude toward non-childbearing which is less than neutral. They happily give contraceptives to a student wife, but any woman over the age of twenty who is married and can have a child without starving to death, has to explain why she wants to prevent conception.

Since men (who run the society) are not relegated to the biological function, women unconsciously, when told to think of themselves as breeding machines, will automatically think of themselves as inferior.

Possibly the greatest contribution from the medical profession to keeping women down (see Chapter VIII) comes from the classical psychoanalysts. Even some women analysts, such as Helene Deutsch, have chosen to interpret Freud (who treated women as equals in his work situation, but treated them as inferiors in his domestic life) in the following manner: any time a woman has aspirations beyond being a wife and mother, she needs help. If she truly was healthy, orgasm, childbirth, nursing, and child-rearing would be enough to keep her happy. The guilt feeling that such idealogy has engendered in women, especially women self-conscious enough to go to psychoanalysts, is enormous. Human aspiration, or rather female aspiration, is discounted. No male is supposed to be fulfilled in life from being a father and a husband; but desires, beyond biological ones, are called sublimation in women. Perhaps, on the contrary, an endless desire for sexual activity might indeed be sublimation from being excluded from all other significant activities in life.

Only the defeated could see themselves as sex objects first. This the psychiatrists recognize in the case of men, but not in the case of women.

In a period when both the "ins" and the "outs" are proclaiming the virtues of love—the "in" psychoanalysts helping people learn how to love in this alienated world, the "in" movie directors describing the horrors of alienation; the "out" hippies loving even the police who beat them on the heads—it is relevant to examine what love means to women. It may indeed be a trap.

In the realm of sexual love, if women confine themselves to one man we are often accused by him, and by the popular press, of driving him to distraction. The newspapers and magazines are full of articles on how the American man simply cannot satisfy his wife sexually. If we spread this love around, we are accused of being promiscuous, which is a sure indication of neurosis, as any doctor or housewife will tell you. When we turn our love to our children, God help us. We are accused of turning our sons into homosexuals, we are accused of smothering our children to death, and we are blamed for everything from driving the children to pot smoking to making their marriages unhappy. Any women past the age of fifteen who still loves her father is accused of having an unresolved Electra complex; if she loves her mother the world knows she is sick and trying to get back to the womb. If a woman is poor and loves a rich man, she is accused of being a gold digger. If she is rich and loves a poor man, she is accused of trying to take it out on poor old Daddy.

Men, at least white middle class men, have a good solution to this love problem. They love themselves. This enables them to enjoy the pleasures of home, children, and wife—and still to achieve in the world.

Rare is the woman who loves herself. This is because we have been taught for 6,000 years that we are the second sex.

The Greeks considered women inferior from birth. For

he thought that a superior woman could outperform a weak man. Aristotle proved from "nature" (and to the satisfaction of his contemporaries) the reasonableness of the social design by which slaves and women, artisans and traders, occupied inevitably a subordinate place. The philosophic opinion of Aristotle about women was in due course confirmed by the Jewish patriarchal tradition, which the Apostles of the Christian faith made the common heritage of Europe. These missionaries from the East confirmed by new religious sanctions the strength of that authority of the male head of the household which had been accepted in ancient Rome. The Christian church, which came to accept so much of its social plan from Plato, substituted for the escape from private ties provided by the Platonic system of a community of wives, the more drastic discipline of the celibacy of the priesthood.

The Oppian law, forbidding luxury to Roman women, was passed at the moment when Hannibal was threatening Rome; once the danger was past, the Roman women demanded that it be repealed. In an oration, Cato demanded its retention, but the appearance of the matrons assembled in the public square overruled him. The Roman Senate finally managed to pass an act forbidding women to enter into contracts with others. The Roman women demonstrated. They swarmed through the streets, besieged the courts; they stirred up civil strife. At the end of the first century and the beginning of the second, we see many women continuing to be the companions and associates of their husbands as they were during the Republic. The laws still forbade adultery, so some matrons had themselves registered as prostitutes in order to facilitate their affairs.

Simone deBeauvoir[3] reports:

"Up to that time Latin literature had always treated women respectfully, but then the satirists were let loose against them. They attacked not women in general, but specifically women of that particular time. Juvenal reproached them for their lewdness and gluttony; he found fault with them for aspiring to men's occupations—they meddled in politics, plunged into the files of legal papers, disputed with grammarians and rhetoricians, went in passionately for hunting, chariot racing, fencing, and wrestling. They were rivals of the men, especially in their taste for amusement and in their vices; they lacked sufficient education to envisage higher aims; and besides, no goal was set up for them—action was still forbidden for them. The Roman woman of the old Republic had a place on earth, but she was chained to it for lack of abstract rights and economic independence; the Roman woman of the decline was the typical product of false emancipation, having only an empty liberty in a world in which men remained in fact the sole master: she was free—but for nothing."

St. Paul ordered women to keep silence in the churches. Tertullian in the second century called us the gate which opened the way to the devil. St. Thomas explained the birth of a female child as a generative mistake.

In Eastern Europe the position of the husband as head of the household was asserted in no uncertain fashion. The priest Sylvester, writing for the admonition of his son during the reign of Ivan the Terrible in the sixteenth century, said:

The husband ought to teach his wife with love and sensible punishment. The wife should ask her husband about all matters of decorum; how to save her soul; how to please husband and God; how to keep the house in good order. And to obey him in everything. . . . And no matter how guilty the wife is, the husband should not hit her eyes or ears, not beat her with his fist or feet under the heart. . . . But to beat carefully with a whip is sensible, painful, fear-inspiring, and healthy. . . . In case of a grave offence, pull off her shirt and whip politely, holding her by the hands and saying: 'Don't be angry; the people should not know about it; there should be no complaints.' "

Apparently the message of Sylvester is still alive and well in Syracuse, New York[4]. A letter to the editor from Ms. X read:

Could someone explain to me what the Women's Liberationists want? I simply can't understand them. In our house my husband's word is law and none of our five children or myself would think of disagreeing with it.

The Almighty meant women to be a helpmate to man, not to compete with him. These liberated ladies better wake up before it's too late. They would have fewer ulcers.

I know my husband is real proud and tells me I look ten years younger than other mothers who are out working in the business world. My children appreciate me too.

I know what contentment means. Home is truly where the heart is.

Lionel Trilling explains, in an essay on Jane Austen, *why* there are no complaints. It is the presumption of our society that women's moral life is not as men's, and that therefore we do not expect from women, in fact do not condone in them, the same degree of self-love which we expect and encourage in men. Since women are in a sense given their lives, since women customarily choose a life-style by choosing a man rather than a path, they do not need the self-love which is necessary to carry a man to the places he has to go. Self-love is indeed a handicap to a being whose primary function is supportive, for how is a woman adequately to support another ego when her self-love demands the primacy of her own?

Having been effectively blocked from achievement in the society, we use a disdain of self-love as a respectable excuse for not attaining goals. In an article in *Woman's Day*, "My Children Keep Me So Tied Down, Thank God," Marion Walker Alcaro writes:

A depressing thought frequently occurs to me. If I had no children, I would have no excuse for not having read all the books on the best-seller lists. . . . I would have no excuse either, it also frequently occurs to me, for not being a more accomplished sportswoman. . . . I would have to keep up with every pronunciamento of Mr. Goren. For I would never, never be able to placate an irate partner with my present standby, "I simply *don't* have time to learn these new conventions!" . . . I would have to be fearfully chic too.

When I first read that article, several years ago, my reaction was that she is an idiot. However, sisterhood and self-love have since caught up with me. Ms. Alcaro is a victim of a culture, writing for other such victims, to defend their mutual plight in life. Her article is a proclamation: Women are supposed to be able to read the books on the best-seller lists. I can't even hack that. My excuse is my children.

Our children are our excuse, and our prison. Mill writes[5]:

All women are brought up from the very earliest years in the belief that their ideal of character is the very opposite to that of men; not self-will, and government by self-control, but submission, and yielding to the control of others. All the moralities tell them that it is the duty of women, and all the current sentimentalities that it is their nature, to live for others; to make complete abnegation of themselves, and to have no life but in their affections. And by their affections are meant the only ones they are allowed to have—those to the men with whom they are connected, or to the children who constitute an additional and indefeasible tie between them and a man.

If the Women's Movement of the 1960s and 70s has taught women one thing, it has taught us self-love and self-respect. It has taught us that no one is going to fight our fight for us. It has taught us that unless we band together, we will never have freedom.

Although our goals are political, the mental health

side-benefits have been enormous. We have the courage to read our history, to see the second-class role we have played in the human drama, and to understand why. We are then free to seek solutions. The solutions cannot be sought alone, with each woman in her kitchen, pounding her fists against the sink. The solutions can be found when we work together.

Once a woman says I am all right—I am even good enough to vote for a woman for President of the United States, to go to a woman doctor, to use the services of a woman attorney—the battle is far from won, but at least it has begun. And from all appearances, we women are now on a collision course with victory.

NOTES TO CHAPTER I

1. Mill, John Stuart, "The Subjection of Women," *Three Essays*. London: Oxford University Press, 1912, Chapter I.
2. Stanlee Miller Coy, *The Single Girl's Book: Making It in the Big City*. Englewood Cliffs, New Jersey: Prentice-Hall, 1969.
3. DeBeauvoir, Simone. *The Second Sex*. Translated and edited by H. M. Parshley. New York, New York: Knopf, 1953, p. 89.
4. *Syracuse Herald-Journal*, June 24, 1970.
5. Mill, *Ibid*.

CHAPTER II

What You Are Taught
in School about Being a Woman

> When a woman inclines to learning there is usually something wrong with her sex apparatus.
> Friedrich Nietzsche, *Beyond Good and Evil* (1886)

You've got to be carefully taught. Who is the football hero? Who is the cheerleader? Girls' conditioning as second-class citizens begins almost before we are born. Daddy wants a boy; Mommy usually does. During the first years of life, boys are taught to be aggressive and self-reliant. Girls are taught to be sweet and loving, to get along with people. We are punished, rather than rewarded, for being "self-starters."

Our toys tell us about our future world, the home. We play with dolls, and toy stoves, and small carpet-sweepers. Our brothers play with toy rocketships, and science kits, and mathematical games.

Kate Millett, in discussing the education of women, points out the role of the school in recapitulating the message[1]:

> When we speak of education for women we have to remember that it begins the moment they are born. The schools only institutionalize the roles which are already established by the time that they are probably one and a half years old. Gender identity is now thought to be established at eighteen months. So that what happens is that the society, the official institutional schools of the society, merely perpetuate the socialization into roles which goes on long before this.

Boys and girls, supposedly educated in the same way, are not. A cynic might argue that they should be educated even more diversely than they are today: given the future role of women it is practically ridiculous to teach philosophy, history, and chemistry. However, the differences in education for boys and girls are subtle.

The undisputed fact that girls do better during the first ten years of school is invariably attributed to the "prissy women school teachers" who teach the lower grades, and reward the girls for keeping the desk neat, writing legibly, and being quiet. The superior performance of female children is never attributed to the fact that, perhaps, they are smarter, or learn faster. The male chauvinist psychologists discuss ad nauseum how harmful it is for the poor little boys to be educated by women teachers, how we need to get more men into the elementary schools.

By the time a girl reaches junior high school, she "discovers" boys, and also discovers the message that a) boys do not like smart girls; and b) her future success is dependent on attracting, catching, and holding one of these boys. Her performance in school falls, and continues to fall through grade 12. If she does still harbor ambitions to be a politician or a scientist, she is systematically counseled by parents and guidance counselors alike that

that is unrealistic: that she should be a school teacher or a clerical worker.

In 1913, Dr. Elizabeth K. Adams wrote: "No part of the history of education is so obscure as that of the education of girls. This obscurity is itself suggestive that little is known because there is little to know."

One thing that every girl senses, even if no one tells her, is that once the pleasures of elementary school are over, we occupy the back of the bus in the educational system. This Southern strategy is described by Mary McGrath[2]:

> Once in a blue moon a girl learns, early in life, just exactly what it is to be a woman. If she accepts the education, her life is immeasurably simpler from that day on.
>
> Well, the moon was blue in a small southern town one day last week. All the girls were moved to the back of the school bus because their presence, scattered among the boys, made the lads so restless they caused trouble.
>
> It may have had nothing to do with the ABC's, or even the so-called three R's, but if that little gambit wasn't relevant education for women, I have never heard better.
>
> It will do the little ladies good to learn early that their place is a respectable number of places in back. It's where they will spend most of their time, anyway. An added bonus in the particular business was also acquiring the knowledge that gentlemen do not get blamed for their own weaknesses, peccadilloes, or peculiarities while there is a gal in the picture upon whom the onus can be shifted.
>
> These kids were only grade school children, but they were subjected to higher education of the most revealing type. If they caught the lesson, it will make them not only more accepting of a lot of future nonsense, but they will be sought after as perfect matches for inconsequential males—of which there seems to be an overabundant supply in every generation.
>
> This single event may be a sign that educators are, at last, getting down to the business of teaching girls to be women with some sense of reality.
>
> The way things are going these days this "Southern

strategy" of female education is liable to sweep the country. These girls will make wonderful wives for the imperfect husbands that the same system will spawn. Of course, they won't be able to think their way out of a paper bag, but that's a real man's dream of a real woman, any day!

Ms. McGrath has illustrated a trend in male = female relations, more significant even than the fact that women are in the back of the bus: this is that when we "disturb" men in some way, the society's answer has been to remove *us*. One reason given for women's not sitting with men in the Orthodox Jewish synagogue is that our presence disturbs the men. The reason given by hotel and restaurant operators all over the United States for prohibiting the admission of unescorted women is that our presence disturbs the men, "makes" them proposition us! If this was not so degrading, it would be thigh-slappingly funny.

When male editors analyze female superior performance, they too, find misogynist reasons. *Parade* magazine[3] ran an article on the superior performance of girls admitted to Yale. "An analysis of first-term grades shows that in the 'honors' category, the coeds outdistanced the men by 27.5% to 23.9%. In the high pass category, 46% of the coeds made the grade compared to 39.6% of the men." The reasons given for this high performance are not that women are smarter, or that perhaps that women who apply to Yale are self-selectedly superior—but "they succumb less to temptation; they practice more discipline; they are better organized; they are basically more competitive when pitted against men; they try harder."

Male reporters[4] also assume that female superior performance is something to fight:

Jersey City, New Jersey—Traditionalists who resist the idea of all-male colleges admitting coeds can find some argument at St. Peter's College.

The Jesuit school admitted its first women students four

years ago, but at commencement exercises Sunday it will be the coeds walking away with most of the academic honors.

Two women will share valedictory honors. Seven will be graduated magna cum laude. No male student will.

College is considered as a place to find a husband (the "good catches" all go to college), or perhaps as a stepping stone to a career as a typist. An ad from the Katharine Gibbs School:

After a girl has spent four years getting a college education it's a shame not to spend just a few more weeks getting ready to qualify for a rewarding job.

College-educated women are needed and wanted in publishing, advertising, communications, finance, and other fascinating fields. Increasingly they are moving up into challenging positions filled with excitement and responsibility.

Many successful women have started out as executive assistants. In that kind of job, you're on the inside of many key decisions. You gain a knowledge of the whole field that can win you a more important position.

BUT—when you go to apply for your first stepping-stone job, you're almost sure to be asked—"How's your typing? Can you take shorthand? Write a decent business letter?"

. . . In just eight weeks, our program will give you enough of the basic office skills that you need to land the kind of job where you can begin to use your college education.

Can you imagine a boy being told that unless he goes to typing school for eight weeks he will not be able to "use his college education"! While male college graduates are entered into executive training programs, female college graduates are made into assistants (secretaries). Only the rare woman ever gets out of this role, so a good piece of advice may indeed be: never tell them you can type, or you will be typing until the day you leave the company.

The reasons for our unequal education, and unequal opportunities following even the best education, are rooted deep in history. "His story" is permeated with definitions of woman's nature, by men:

Lord Chesterfield said:

> Women, then, are only children of larger growth; they have an entertaining rattle and sometimes wit; but not solid reasoning, or good sense. I never knew in my life one that had it or one who reasoned or acted consequently for four and twenty hours altogether. . . .
>
> A man of sense only trifles with them, plays with them, humors and flatters them, as he does a sprightly forward child; but he neither consults them, nor trusts them with serious matters; though he often makes them believe that he does, which is the thing in the world that they are most proud of . . .
>
> Women are much more like each other than men; they have in truth but two passions, vanity and love; these are their universal characteristics.

These often-quoted generalizations, as Gordon Allport has pointed out, contain familiar expressions of prejudice which are habitually used against an out-group. Just as some Europeans used to say that all Chinese looked alike, so Chesterfield generalizes about women, insisting we all think alike. His condescending description is similar to the image which the die-hard segregationist applies to the black person or the white-man's-burden imperialist to a colonial people.

Lord Kames[6] discussed our role in life. "Women destined by nature to be obedient, ought to be disciplined early to bear wrongs without murmuring. . . . To make a good husband is but one branch of a man's duty, but it is the chief duty of a woman to make a good wife."

Between 1781 and 1970 views on the education of women have been but slightly revised. In "How to Get and Hold a Woman,"[7] a marriage counselor explains how "it goes against a woman's nature to work, but she will gladly slave to take care; by herself woman is all mixed-up but superb as an auxiliary; woman is inanimate or on the defensive until you create a feeling such as a praise (then she goes all out); women act only on orders, . . . so these had better be yours." The author tells us that "the acquisition of knowledge or responsibilities does not lessen women's need for support, guidance, and control. . . . Why ask women, when they only need to be told? Why ask women when they hope to be taken?"

In the field of education, our position has been going steadily down. In 1930, women made up 30% of college faculties; today, 22%. Twenty years ago nearly all elementary school principals were women; today, only 37%. This, incidentally, is part of the "upgrading" of the education profession. (It should be observed that as part of the so-called upgrading of the social work and library science professions, women were removed from most of their positions of power, as administrators in the field and as heads of training institutions. These fields now command more status and more money; they are now run by men.)

In 1930 women earned 40% of master's degrees; currently 34%. Women's doctorates are down from 15% in 1930 to 12%. In the professions, twenty-five years has seen women decline from 45% to 37%. In politics, the 87th Congress included nineteen women; the 93rd has thirteen women. Women in state legislatures declined from 370 to 318 in two years.[8]

In the *Academic Woman*,[9] Jessie Bernard quotes from an interview with a male patient in a hospital:

> For the first time in my life, I think I can begin to understand what it must feel like to be a woman. . . . To have to wangle favors from more powerful people, like nurses. To be dependent on brisk, competent, though inferior, attendants. To be hemmed in, robbed of autonomy, because if you displease people they can just physically

overpower you and put you back in your place. This experience has changed my whole personality. . . . I was never condescended to, patronized, before. I have to resist the attitude of the nurses or I become like a child. I become devious. I have to outwit them by strategy, since I don't have either the physical strength or hospital rules on my side. The whole situation has affected even my relations with the two other men in the room. We feel and act like conspirators. Even our logic was affected. The nurses behaved according to the logic of hospital rules, which seemed to us to be all in their favor. If a few weeks of being without superior strength and the support of the rules can do this to a man, what can years of it do to a woman?

Dr. Ann Scott, Assistant Professor of English at the State University of New York (Buffalo), has written a report, *The Half-Eaten Apple: A Look at Sex Discrimination in the University,* which documents what lack of superior strength, and mainly, no support *from the rules,* has done to women in higher education.

Although Eve's bite into that apple made her the world's first seeker after higher learning, her fate was to be punished for her presumption, rather than praised for her initiative. . . . Since Eve, women's academic progress has been largely downhill. From its invention in Athens until the nineteenth century, higher education has remained a man's world from which women were resolutely barred, and the change came about only because women themselves insisted on their right to learn. Yet even as late as 1907, the German scientific encyclopedist P. Moebius could state that "extraordinarily important parts of the brain necessary for spiritual life, the frontal convolutions and the temporal lobes, are less well developed in women, and this difference is inborn. . . . That the sciences, in the strictest sense, have received no enrichment from women and never shall is therefore understandable."

These ideas were seriously discussed by a generation of men, in their fight against women's suffrage.

Dr. Scott found that "A sad fact is that while universities in 1970 have made genuine efforts on behalf of the other minority groups, they are no freer of the traditional attitudes toward women than any other group in our society. We are barely present in the faculties of coeducational institutions, and even in the women's colleges are concentrated in the lower levels. . . . Rank reveals an inverse spiral: the higher the academic stratum, the lower the overall percentage of women, until at the summit women simply evaporate."

The absence of women in the university faculty and administration is a clear case of employment discrimination. However, even more harmful to women, is that this creates an absence of role models for the girl students. When a woman students thinks about scholars and university professors and college presidents, she cannot possibly think that these jobs apply to her.

Dr. Scott collected the figures on women in her university. While women comprised 50% of the freshman class, they represent only 21% of the graduate students, 14% of the faculty, and only 5% of the full professors. In department after department, overwhelmingly male faculties are earning their livings out of what has been called "the pimping system." They train women into professions in which they are unwilling to hire women as colleagues and equals. All this, of course, in an institution supported totally by public funds.

The formal sexism in the university takes place in hiring teachers and administrators, in salary differentials, in tenure policy, and in giving financial aid to students. Of the forty-three departments of SUNY at Buffalo, for example, seventeen have no women faculty and twenty-two have no tenured women faculty members. Tenured women are 5% of the total faculty, compared to 50% for men. The figures at SUNY/Buffalo are typical for the

universities in this country. In an analysis of administrative salaries, the average is $200 a year more for men
with no degree; $400 more for men with bachelor's de-
grees; and $1200 more for men with master's degrees.

The university is consistent with the rest of society,
where women with three years of college earn less than
men with an eighth grade education.

One factor discriminates very heavily against women
in higher education: this is the total lack of university
responsibility for providing child-care facilities. Every
male—undergraduate, graduate student, or faculty member—who is a parent, has a child-care center: his wife.
The females are not so fortunate, however.

Recruiting and hiring of women faculty members is
made especially difficult because of the nepotism or
"favoritism" rule, whereby universities deny employment
to the spouses and relatives of faculty employees. In
practice, this almost never prevents the husband from
getting an appointment. It has caused, however, among
academic women, countless cases of superior highly
qualified women being denied employment in their profession because they have followed their husband, also
an academic, to a university town where they cannot be
hired.

The most insidious form of sex discrimination in the
university occurs in the course content. Learning that
women are not equal begins in the elementary school.
It is of course most dangerous when taught to small girls;
but at the university level, all this high-powered sexist
learning takes on the remarkableness, the distinction, of
the university. It becomes science. Dr. Scott writes: "Many
disciplines, particularly in the social sciences, teach the
traditional sex roles as if they were holy truths rather
than the result of cultural conditioning. By this I do not
mean to say that the ideas of Bruno Bettelheim or Erik

Erikson or Sigmund Freud should not be taught, but that their male orientation must be clearly labeled, so that students—men as well as women—will know that they are being taught theories, not facts."

Women in academia have not been uniformly loyal to their sex. Since most of the women who have "made it" are so grateful to be there, and have had to work so very hard to be where they are, they tend to consider themselves what Betty Friedan calls "another sex." [These women, she contends, think that there are three sexes: men, and most women (who enjoy the pleasures of the kitchen), and then another kind of women like themselves—imaginative, creative, successful.] These women either accept the male chauvinist values of the university, or else parrot these values without believing them, because they know that their own success depends to a large degree on not making trouble. The result of this is that you will still find women psychologists, for example, participating in a symposium where it is stated that women like to be dominated, are naturally more gentle, and so forth.

A study by the Women's Caucus for Political Science of the American Political Science Association found, in 1970, that there were 628 full professors (male) and 25 full professors (female) at UCLA; at Stanford there were 490 male full professors and 8 female full professors. At the other end of the pyramid, there were 266 male lecturers and 86 female lecturers at UCLA, and 89 male lecturers and 30 female lecturers at Stanford. Although men outnumber women at all the academic ranks, it is apparent that the women who are in academia tend to be at the bottom of the ranking scale.

A study of 240 American universities by the University of Wisconsin (1970) shows that they discriminate against women in college admissions. "At the low ability level, males were preferred over females. At the higher ability levels, this difference disappeared. Since in the high school population, there are more students, both male and female, at the lowest of our ability levels than at higher levels, it is clear that, overall, women are discriminated against in college admission." These findings also fit into the general pattern in American culture that superior women usually can "make it," but that average women are not given the same opportunities as their male peers—the average male.

"As the situation stands today, both forms of education for women [coeducational colleges, women's colleges] have failed. Both the segregated and the integrated patterns have proven incompetent in providing women with the incentive for a true higher education and professional participation." This is the conclusion drawn by Kate Millett.[10] She found that while the coeducational institutions were definitely keyed to educating males, not necessarily females, the all-female schools themselves accepted the role of women as wife and mother, and even the "top" women's schools did not consider their major task to be the intellectual and professional development of the student.

The Mount Holyoke catalog, for example, discusses service rather than achievement. "Today thousands of alumnae, in every part of the world, are serving their families and their communities with generosity and imagination, leading lives that enrich those they touch, ready to meet the unknown with steadiness and gaiety."

That these women do not feel so steady and gay is well described by Mary McCarthy, in *The Group*. That best-selling novel puts the feminine mystique on the stage, and shows what happens to women who have been educated at first-rate women's colleges—taught philosophy and history—and then are consigned to breast-feeding and gourmet cooking. They are, to say the least, an un-happy bunch.

Most women's colleges, however, are not at the eastern-girls-school level. *Token Learning* quotes at length from the catalog of the Texas Women's College—"a state-supported institution providing calculatedly inferior education for women":

> What better preparation could there be for marriage that nursing? All that you learn of child-care, nutrition, psychology, medicines, treatments and of dealing tactfully with people will be wonderfully useful to you whether you marry or not. Everything you learn in nursing stands by you through life; you have confidence in your knowledge of what to do in case of illness or accident, and nursing is a career you can combine successfully with marriage.
>
> Homemaking—the greatest career of all for women—is a science and an art. Home economics is unique in being the only area of higher education which simultaneously trains its students to fill the role of homemaker while also preparing them for professional careers. Home economics education has as one of its goals the training of girls to become excellent wives and mothers and happy members of a family group. Teachers with creative ideas, enthusiasm, good judgment and homemaking skills find their profession highly satisfying.

Kate Millett says: "Texas Women's is anxious to encourage its students to enter the masculine field of "physics," wherefore it has found the novel argument that physics produces better wives." The Texas Women's catalog:

"Less than 3% of American physicists are women. This fact is unfortunate, because it represents a considerable loss of potential scientific brainpower. American girls should realize that, if they wish, they can combine home-making more satisfactorily with a career in science than with many other conventional careers. This fact is particularly true for the woman scientist who marries a scientist, since she is already familiar with the scientific intensity, the scientific hours, and the scientific language. This is also particularly true for the woman who wishes to teach science, since there is nearly always an opening in the local high school for a good science teacher. A woman who makes her career in physics can look forward to a lifetime of rewarding professional satisfaction, whether it be in industry or in education or in the home."

Law school apparently is also a school for wives. Ms. Rogers, wife of the Secretary of State, is an honor graduate from Cornell University Law School. She has never practiced law, and has been quoted several times as saying that it is an advantage for a lawyer (Mr. Rogers) to be married to a lawyer (her), because she can better understand his work!

I attended Northwestern University School of Journalism during the height of the feminine mystique (1955–59). I was counseled by family, friends, and professors to go into elementary education, because "I would be home when my children came home from school." In journalism school, everyone had a major outside of the professional course. Mine was history and sociology. Every woman was told to major in home economics because "that was where the jobs were." My friends were for the most part in elementary education. Every one of us was conscious of how the boys in our life would react to our chosen professions. We attempted at all times to be nonthreatening: not to discuss our intended careers with our dates. One friend of mine, with an excellent business sense and enormous efficiency, was in the School of Commerce, which was a training ground for junior executives (male) all over the world. She was counseled into becoming a teacher of typing and shorthand. Another friend, in the journalism school, took a job eventually in a writing capacity, but in her husband's field, so she "would better understand his work." If a Northwestern graduate wanted to work on a Chicago newspaper, he had to work for one year at the City News Bureau, an agency which covered local news for all the newspapers. I say "he" because no woman could get a job on the City News Bureau at that time; the only route to working on a Chicago paper was to work in a small town on the woman's page, and then come to the big city, to work on the woman's page. Another friend went through law school with her husband, getting higher grades than he, and then became a housewife, while he is a successful lawyer.

It must be pointed out that to get into Northwestern in 1955 you had to be at the very top of your high school class. Despite the academic (and possibly intellectual) excellence of my friends, I cannot think of *one* of us who had any plans for herself. We all knew we had to get married, if not at 20, at 23 after a nervous three years of old maidhood.

Certain areas of female leadership are disappearing in recent years. Fred Hechinger reports[11] that "in the top management of American higher education, women's opportunities are declining. Female presidents of the women's colleges have been replaced by men in what looks like a steady trend. . . . Male presidents, taking the national women's college scene as a whole, have long been the rule rather than the exception. But until recently the presidency, particularly in some of the Big Seven women's colleges . . . has been regarded as a key spot in which strong and able women could make their mark, not only on campus but on intellectual society at large. . . . In recent years, the women have been crowded out of the contest. Among the Big Seven, only Wellesley, Barnard and Radcliffe remain under female leadership.

Even this overstates the remaining female power: Barnard is closely connected with the male-dominated Columbia and Radcliffe has recently expressed its desire to be completely merged with Harvard which already controls its curricular affairs." Mr. Hechinger closes with "the saying 'May the best man win' will mean just that in the academic contest."

Government figures indicate that even a high degree of education and training does not necessarily bring the average woman a salary comparable to a man's. In 1968, for example, a woman with four years of college was typically earning $6,694 a year, while a man with an eighth-grade education averaged $6,580. The typical male college graduate, meanwhile, earned $11,795. A recent survey by Frank S. Endicott, placement director of Northwestern University[12] shows no change. Average starting salaries offered by major firms in all fields were higher for men than women.

As for the 150 companies studied by ASPA and BNA, 97% of those doing any campus recruiting went to coed campuses; 63% to all-male campuses; only 30% to the women's colleges.

Judging what happens to women when we try to use our college educations, it is perhaps the height of cynical realism to go directly from the campus to the kitchen: you know you can't make it out there in the world anyway.

Girls experience discrimination in getting into college. Women are turned away from colleges and universities with higher scores on tests and high school grades than men who are accepted. This is in part because of the quota system which prefers men. At Stanford, for example, they have two males for every female student. At MIT, they have 5,000 male undergraduates; 250 females In the State University of New York system they have different standards of admission for men and women.

One reason which has been cited for having stricter standards of admission for female students is that the women are more qualified (do better in high school), so that if the universities let in women on the basis of merit, we would overcrowd the institutions of higher education!

Women's liberation groups all over the country have been filing formal discrimination complaints, and have held up Federal contracts at 2,000 colleges and universities. The Women's Equity Action League (WEAL) filed against the University of Miami. The National Organization for Women (NOW) has filed against Harvard University (holding up $46 million in federal government contracts), the University of Pittsburgh, and the State University of New York (SUNY). A Caucus on Women's Rights at SUNY was formed in summer 1970 to demand equality for women within the state university system.

Women college students have also been protesting their second-class status. About forty of Yale's new coeds invaded the Alumni Day luncheon (February 21, 1970) with clenched fists and placards and protested the ratio of women to men in the student body (300 to 4,000).

A group of women faculty members at Columbia University issued a report (spring 1970) charging discrimination against women in that university's hiring policies. The report noted, among other things, that Columbia grants about 25% of its doctoral degrees to women students, that only 2% of the tenured faculty members are women. George Fraenkel, dean of Columbia's Graduate Faculties, told the *New York Times:* "There is no overt, conscious antiwoman attitude in the university's hiring policies . . . [but] a tenured position requires a tremendous amount of dedication and time that interferes with our normal idea of a woman's role in the family."

The "normal" idea of a woman's role in the family is parroted by many women too. Women still feel that they must play down their abilities or they will ruin their matrimonial chances. About 40% of a group of female college students interviewed in 1943 believed that they must play dumb or they would frighten men. In 1958, an investigator was told by a department store executive: "A woman should not try to get ahead of the men at any time. They'll only buck her and give her trouble, but if you work with them and sort of take the attitude that he [sic] who is humble shall be exalted and so forth, you'll make out much better."

In the last few years I have talked to hundreds of high school and college girls. With the exception of those who have gained self-love through the movement, most women still believe that men want them docile, and that attracting men is their primary function in life.

In addition, it is "understood" that there are girls' fields and boys' fields. Females are systematically told they will not be good in mathematics and science; the average trigonometry class in high school has one or two girls in it. Kate Millett writes in *Token Learning:* "Those subjects of study which are given the highest status in American life are 'masculine,' those given the lowest are 'feminine.' Thus, math, the sciences of biology, chemistry, and physics, business administration, architecture, medicine and law are 'men's subjects,' and the humanities are relegated with a philistine contempt to the level of something 'suitable to women.' For some inscrutable reason French, Art History, and English literature are ladylike, although academically respectable, and the brightest young women are carefully screened into them."

So thoroughly have female students been trained, they participate in self-hate by assuming that the male teacher/scholar knows more. The John/Joan McKay study proved not only that men think more highly of male scholars than female, but that females do. Two groups of students were given a learned article to evaluate. One group received the article signed "Joan McKay," the other signed "John McKay." John McKay impressed the students as a good scholar; Joan McKay did not.

The male philosophers have often identified our problem, but they cannot be expected to protest it. That is our job. Paul Goodman[13] writes about the boys of today: "I say the young men and boys because the problems I want to discuss in this book belong primarily in our society to boys: how to be useful and to make something of oneself. A girl does not have to; she is not expected to make something of herself. Her career does not have to be self-justifying, for she will have children, which is absolutely self-justifying like any other natural or creative act. With this background, it is less important, for instance, what job an average young woman works at till she is married."

Bruno Bettelheim sees the confused message given to female children:[14]

> Consider the contradictions which are thus thrust upon the growing girl. For fifteen years or more she is officially encouraged to compete with boys in the schoolroom, to develop her mind and her initiative, to be second to none. She may study the same physics and history as her boyfriends, work at jobs not too different from theirs, share many of the same political and social interests. And then our curious system insists she 'fall in love' with a potential husband; she is in fact expected to love giving up what she may have loved until then, and suddenly find deep fulfillment in taking care of a child, a home, a mate—the training of her youth is seemingly intended to fall away like an afterbirth.

The boys have no doubt that their schooling is intended, at least, to help them make a *success* in their mature life, to enable them to accomplish something in the outside world. But the girl is made to feel that she must undergo precisely the same training only because she may need it if she is a *failure*—an unfortunate who somehow cannot gain admission to the haven of marriage and motherhood where she properly belongs. Surely this is absurd.

When Chancellor Kimpton spoke to *Time* magazine about his plans for the reorganization of the University of Chicago (in the 50s) he said it was going to become the school for the boy who wanted to make a million dollars, and the girl who wanted to marry him. In the University of Denver admissions brochure (1970) which describes coeducational dormitory living, the administrators have written: "if you are lucky you can find a girl to iron your shirts." At Queens College in New York, a student cannot stay on if she is pregnant.

There is, however, hope for women. Cornell, Vassar, Radcliffe, Wells College, Oberlin, Princeton, and San Diego State are planning Women's Studies programs. Many schools offer courses on the role of women. Dr. Joy Osofsky teaches the course at Cornell: Human Development and Family Studies 390. It includes material on the relative position of women in the United States to other countries, the legal status of women, socialization and sex role development, marriage, and women in literature. Dr. Marguerite Fisher is teaching a course on Women in the American Democracy at Syracuse University. The course includes the historical background of the women's rights movement and an examination of the status and problems of American women today, including comparative family structures and personality development.

Commencement speeches in June 1970, included many that are hopeful signs for the future of women. At Tully Central School (New York), Margaret Murphy spoke on women's rights. She had become aware that we were lacking them when she was told that the Veterinary School at Cornell University, which she wanted to attend, only lets in one girl each year; one reason given was that girls cannot lift the 500-pound cows (presumably the male student can!). Her speech described how girls who are superior in science are counseled to be nurses, how girls who excel in human relations are encouraged into kindergarten teaching (their male counterparts are directed to medicine, physics, psychiatry). The most dangerous thing about the brainwash is what it does to you: "By the time you graduate, *you* think you want to be a nurse, or a kindergarten teacher, or a wife and mother."

For the first time in Harvard's history, the graduates of Radcliffe received their diplomas along with the men in June 1970. And, also for the first time, the traditional commencement address in Latin was delivered by a woman, Kirstèn Mishkin, a *magna cum laude* graduate. She spoke perfect Latin, about the glory of our past, but more significant, about the task we must perform in the future.

> Rejoice, O women of old! O brave and unconquered—Susan B. Anthony, Elizabeth Cady Stanton, Elizabeth Blackwell, Elizabeth Agassiz—who struggled courageously for suffrage, for womanly dignity, for an education and training for girls which would be equal to that of boys. At Harvard University, in America, in the world, woman's position is widely recognized to be inferior. Women have learned to despise themselves. Resources, opportunities and honors available to men are denied women. . . . Not yet can we lay down our weapons, my sisters, nor must we abandon so long and difficult a battle. Everywhere an iniquitious male supremacy is rampant.

But not for long.

NOTES TO CHAPTER II

1. Proceedings, Cornell Conference on Women, January 22–25, 1969.
2. *The Miami Herald*, July 2, 1970.
3. July 5, 1970
4. Associated Press, May 31, 1970.
5. *New York Times*, June 6, 1970.
6. *Loose Hints Upon Education*, 1781.
7. Montreal, Canada: G. C. Payette, 1970.
8. These figures from Dr. Edith G. Painter, dean of women at Youngstown, Ohio, State University.
9. Pennsylvania State University Press, 1967, pp. 168–69.
10. Millett, Kate. *Token Learning: A Study of Women's Higher Education in America*. New York: National Organization for Women, 1968.
11. *New York Times*, August 24, 1969.
12. Reported in *U.S. News and World Report*, April 13, 1970.
13. Goodman, Paul. *Growing Up Absurd*, New York: Random House, 1956, p. 13.
14. "Growing Up Female," *Harper's Magazine*, October, 1962, pp. 121–28.

CHAPTER III

Textbooks: "Look Jane, look!
See Dick run and jump!
Admire him!"

*I*N CASE the image of women has not been totally in-
stilled in a little girl before she is five years old, by television and by her parents and friends, school finishes the
job. Teachers are individuals, and school curriculum varies
from locale to locale, so it can be argued that there is no
uniform content. However, one crucial item in the edu-
cative process is standard: the textbook.

Today there are about fifteen major textbook companies
which control about 90% of the textbook market. They
watch each other closely and produce very similar products. And they have the image of woman as helpmate,
as mother, as *observer* of male activities, included in every
book. School attendance is compulsory in this country.
This means that every young girl *must* read about herself as passive citizen for twelve years—by law.

As a former textbook editor I was aware of this image,
but I did not know how prevalent it was until I studied[1]

textbooks, grades Kindergarten through 3. I did a content analysis of social studies books and readers put out by ten companies. In this group of textbooks, no women worked outside the home except as a teacher or a nurse. The teachers and nurses were Miss, indicating clearly that when a woman marries she leaves her profession. This in spite of the fact that over half the women in the United States are employed outside the home; one-third of the women with pre-school children work; and 40% of the mothers of school-age children are employed.

No man was shown as doing anything except going to work outside the home, as a full-time occupation. None were students, none were unemployed, none did housework, except "men's work" such as gardening and taking out the garbage.

The *decision-making* for the family was done by men. This included decisions about household matters. For example, in one story, the children want to build a sandbox. They are told by the mother (the full-time mother) to wait and ask father how to do it when he gets home.

Girls do most of the work helping mother: washing the dishes, caring for the baby, setting the table, etc. Boys also help mother, but father does not. The clear implication is that when the boy grows up he will be a father, and not do the work of women and children. In one story the family has a new baby and everyone is chipping in to "help mother" with "her" work. Father is carrying the laundry, but the poor man cannot manage it. He stumbles and trips and laundry spills out of the basket. The children say "Poor Father." Here we are supposed to believe that an adult male, who presumably earns enough money to support a family of five, does not have what it takes to get the laundry done. The lesson is clearly that father may help out in an emergency, but his job is not keeping the clothes clean.

The youngest child (usually female) is always saved from danger by the oldest child (always male). Father provides all the good times for the family, and also solves the problems. In one story, the family is going on a car trip (100 miles) to visit Grandmother and Grandfather. Mother says wait until Father comes home. He will read his map (the implication is that she doesn't do that big intellectual stuff), and plan how to make the trip (100 miles down the superhighway). The family is pictured sitting around father, watching him plan the trip. In textbook illustrations, whenever the whole family is in the car, *father always is driving*, with mother sitting by his side.

Despite the fact that many mothers work outside the home, the mothers in the textbooks (ideals) are at home. One story[2] shows a little boy coming home from school. "Where is Mother?" The implication is that at three o'clock in the afternoon every woman has to be at home. The child shows signs of anxiety when he does not see his mother around. He goes into the kitchen and sees the pots steaming. He says that he knows mother is at home. We know what mother does at home. She doesn't make pottery, or snooze on the couch. She cooks, at three o'clock in the afternoon. In addition to the idea that mother must be home at all times, is the suggestion that children are not encouraged to be autonomous. These stories take place in the suburbs, where it is certainly safe for a child to play without finding his mother.

Mother is cooking in contemporary stories; she is also cooking in social studies textbooks about cave life. Daddy is also out working (shooting animals?) in those days. In the more modern stories, Daddy comes driving home in his red car. The children run out to greet him. "Daddy works. Daddy works and Bobby works. Bobby works at school and mother works at home."

In a social studies textbook[3] the children are shown pictures of persons in various occupations. Each group consists of three white and two black persons. The text says: "Here are some clothes that tell us what kind of work people do. Look at the pictures and see if you can tell what kind of work these people do." The nurses are *all female;* the doctors are *all male.* In current discussions about unisex clothing, it has been said that it is too confusing for middle America: You don't want to mistake a man for a woman for the same reason that you don't want to mistake the chairman of the board for the janitor. In the textbooks, no such mistakes can be made.

When the textbooks go outside the family and teach about the outer world, the sex stereotyping is the same. The publishers can defend, of course, by saying that they portray the real world as it is. They can't show women in the space program—we aren't in the space program. They can't show women on the Supreme Court—as the second printing of this book went to press, President Nixon was being urged to nominate the first woman to the Court. An appropriate answer to this would be to point to what happened to the portrayal of black people in the textbooks when the 1966 Federal Executive Order came out saying that there would be no federal money available for textbooks in any school district unless the textbooks were integrated—and showed black people in roles other than porter and maid.

"The concessions of the privileged to the unprivileged are seldom brought about by any better motive than the power of the unprivileged to extort them."[4]

Most money for textbooks comes, directly or indirectly, from the federal government. So, the publishers got busy and blackened faces. This presented all kinds of problems: How can you put black people in the suburbs when they don't live there? Can you portray the typical black person's life in a textbook? These problems were not solved, but were attacked by creating Urban Life series, and also by showing life as it *should* be—that is, integrated.

The point to be made is that when women demand that we be shown in roles other than Mommy baking the cake, it will happen. Until we demand it, we will never be shown as functioning persons in the society, and the young girls will learn, right along with learning to read, that their reading in later years can be confined to cookbooks. No one sat around the Office of Education in 1966 and said "I think there is a bad image of black people in the textbooks. All black children will grow up thinking they must be domestic servants." The change came because black people themselves developed a bit of self-love and demanded that their children be given fair treatment in the public school reading materials.

Another area of unfairness to women in textbooks is that we are effectively written out of history. It is obvious that because of being constantly pregnant (there was no contraception until recently) and mainly because of the oppressive culture that has kept women down, women have not "made" history to as great an extent as men. (The women Presidents of the United States have not been kept out of the history books; they don't exist.) In addition, there has been a tendency, because men run political systems (and also write history) to value the kinds of contributions which men make and devalue the kinds of contributions which women make. Nonetheless, women have played many important roles in history, and these are missing from the textbooks. For example, an American history textbook contains one paragraph (two sentences) on the women suffrage movement in the United States.

If it is dangerous for little girls to read about Mother who is always in the kitchen cooking (and never in the world, being an architect or doctor or plumber), if it is dangerous for little girls to read stories about heroes, with never a heroine—the most harmful of all is for them to read about how young boys and young girls do different things, even at age three.

In an exclusive nursery school in Washington, D.C., parents are told, during their initial tour, about the fine equipment. They are shown the playroom for the little boys: space suits, construction equipment, and mathematical toys. The playroom for little girls contains toy stoves, toy irons, and dolls.

In the textbooks, the boys take the initiative. They decide what to play, they are the leaders. They are also more creative. One story shows a boy and a girl walking through the forest. The boy is eagerly looking for new plants; the girl is afraid she will see a snake, and is clutching on to his hand. The standard illustration is of boys *doing* something (climbing, running, investigating) and girls *watching* them, sometimes silently and sometimes with enthusiasm (the forerunner of the cheerleader who roots for the football team).

This portrayal in the textbooks actually goes against the research, which shows that until the junior high school level, the females excel in almost everything. At puberty, the boys catch up, and then excel in scholastic skills for the rest of their lives. One explanation of this is that the boys have caught up physically. Another explanation is that at puberty the girls get the message that they aren't supposed to win, and so they stop winning.

A story on class elections, written to teach the democratic process, shows a boy as class president, a girl as class secretary. Another girl says: "Bobby, that isn't fair. I'd like to be president. Everyone should have a chance." But she is elected secretary.[5]

The oppression of women in the textbook field occurs

not only in content, but in form. Just as most school teachers are women, but the administrators are men, a high percentage of editors and writers of children's textbooks are women. But publishing houses are run almost exclusively by men. And this is what they choose to tell young girls about themselves.

An essay[6] by Elizabeth Fisher in the *New York Times* Book Section investigated books for young children in bookstores and libraries and found "an almost incredible conspiracy of conditioning. Boys' achievement drive is encouraged; girls' is cut off. Boys are brought up to express themselves; girls to please. The general image of the female ranges from dull to degrading to invisible."

She found that (although females comprise 51% of the population of the United States) they appear in only 20–30% of picture books. There were five times as many males in the titles as females, four times as many boys, men, or male animals pictured as there were females. Animals are males, for the most part. In the veld, it is the female lion who does all the work; in the picture-book world, she doesn't exist.

Ms. Fisher points out that things are so bad for women in children's story books that one has to go to the Old Testament for an upgrading of the female:

> Only in Noah's Ark does Biblical authority enforce equal representation for males and females. Except for Random House's "Pop-up Noah," which has eliminated Mrs. Noah and does not show animals in equal distribution on the cover—males have a slight edge of course. The wives of Ham, Shem, and Japheth, present in the Old Testament, were missing from all three children's versions I examined.

Sesame Street, produced by National Educational Television, is universally recognized as a first-rate and pioneering series which is far ahead of its times in terms of educational method and social philosophy. One of its stated goals is to socialize children, hopefully many of them "disadvantaged" children who can raise their self-images by identifying with persons on the program. The key target for self love is the young black male. For this reason (so said the directors in an interview) it was decided not to do much with the females on the program. We are supposed to know that the black male suffers from too much matriarchy. On the show, sex differences are strongly emphasized. "Who combs your fur? Does Daddy comb your fur? No, Daddy goes to work. Mommy combs my fur." The women on the program either stay at home or work at traditional female jobs. (One female was at home and then decided to enter the health professions—as a nurse, rather than as a doctor. She returned to her former profession—nursing—only after cajoling her disgruntled husband into agreeing.) The series, which is leading the educational profession in teaching mathematics to pre-school children, perpetuates the same stereotypic myths about women that existed in educational materials 100 years ago. The series which is creating self-love in black male children isn't doing the same for female children of any race.

The marked absence of females in children's books applies even more strongly to books about blacks. Despite the growing number of children's stories about young black boys, Ms. Fisher could only find one about a black girl.

Virginia Woolf pointed out that throughout literature women were shown only in relation to men; this is still true in picture books. Friendship between boys is much touted; friendship between boys and girls is frequent; but friendship between girls gets less attention, despite real life, where young girls spend most of their time with their girl friends.

There is one thing we all learn very early about our

friendships with girls. This is that they take second place to any relationship with a male. If one has a date to do something with a girl, and the chance for a date with a *boy* comes along, the whole world expects the former to be broken. Friendship of female and female is appropriately not much mentioned in the children's books, for this bonding has never been considered important in the world. We women are competitors: we compete for the best men, we compete to have the most lovely clothes, we compete to be the most beautiful. Women are supposed to hate beautiful women. All this is not accidental; it has two important political implications. The first is that women are important only in their relationships to men. A single girl is nothing; marriage is the goal. If no man wants you, you are no good. The second is more subtle: divide and conquer. As long as women do not band together there is little chance of our getting any power, and changing our status. So, the bridge club is highly acceptable in our culture, as long as the talk stays on trumps and jello molds. Discussion of the realities of the wife's life to her friends, for example, is called "disloyal." Disloyal to the male culture. (A wife who killed her husband in medieval days was not prosecuted for murder, but rather for *treason.*)

Ms. Fisher says that since there are so few females in the books, one would think they'd be very busy, but such is not the case. "What they do is highly limited." What they do *not* do is more telling. They do not drive cars. They do not work, as women do in this country, as executives (few, but they exist), jockeys, college professors, lawyers, stockbrokers, taxi drivers, steelworkers, and physicians. Girls in the books are passive. They walk, read, or dream.

One exception is *Mommies at Work*, by Eve Merriam. Although it describes mothers who split atoms and are writers, it is highly apologetic, closing with: ". . . all Mommies loving the best of all to be your very own Mommy and coming home to you."

Both the textbooks and the fiction for children show male involvement with things and activities, and female involvement with emotions. Boys balance in the tree; girls watch. Boys fish, boys roll in leaves, boys hang from ropes, boys climb, boys make scientific discoveries, boys plant trees. Girls watch—the activities, and the baby. In a book showing an orchestra of twenty-eight animals, the two females are playing (as usual) the harp and the piano.

Until we female authors, editors, teachers, and parents refuse to perpetuate the myths of ourselves as fawning observers, Mommy will always be at home, or at the very best, she will come home from a job and say she really prefers her role as mother to that of college professor.

With the current selection of reading material available for young children, I would suggest that it would be much better for the minds and the spirits of a young girl to-day not to learn to read at all, than to read about how she is a passive and emotional observer in the world of the male. Better for her mind, because she would ob-serve her natural equality and not have to read about her inequality. Better for her spirit, because it is obvious that if nobody tells a little girl she is a second-class citizen her instinctive self-love will carry her ahead in the world.

This is not a plea for anti-intellectualism. It is however a demand for an end to the cruel and unusual punish-ment suffered by a little girl reading about herself in children's literature.

NOTES TO CHAPTER III

1. Paper presented at the Susan B. Anthony Conference on Women, sponsored by NOW, Syracuse, New York, February 14, 1970, "You've Got to be Carefully Taught."
2. *We Play*, Hunnicutt, et al, L. W. Singer, 1963, pp. 37–39.
3. *Exploring Our Needs*, Rita Goldman, Follett Publishing Company, Chicago, 1967, p. 88.
4. John Stuart Mill, Ibid.
5. Conscious effort is being made to change this pattern. On October 30, 1970, a new national organization was formed, its first chapter in Syracuse, New York: The Future Politicians of America is to train girls in elementary, junior high, and high school for a role as politicians in school politics, in preparation for college politics, and national politics. Up until this time, such organizations were Future Teachers of America, Future Homemakers of America, and Future Secretaries of America. The national director is Carol E. Singer.
6. Fisher, Elizabeth. "The Second Sex, Junior Division," May 24, 1970, *New York Times* Book Section, p. 6.

CHAPTER IV

Sanctified Slavery:
What You Are Taught in Sunday
School about Being a Woman

ALTHOUGH MANY thorough Biblical scholars, some of them women, have proved that the Bible is not anti-female, it is clear that most accepted interpretations of the Bible place women in a second caste. More important, the experience of women in the churches has been that of second-class citizens.

The special danger of what you learn at Sunday School about being a woman is that this information has the patina of the word of God, and hence, is perhaps more damaging to a woman than when (say) the Board of Education deems that girl students cannot have any money for their after-school sports. And, even among those Americans who are not religious and who do not go to Church, the basic dogma of the Judaic-Christian tradition has permeated their thinking; we are all products of Western civilization—and the second-class role of women in Western civilization is indeed sanctified (and often created) by the Judaic-Christian tradition.

Jewish women cannot read from the Torah. Christian doctrine clearly considers women in a second-class position to men, much as men occupy that position vis à vis God. Women are not ordained as priests or rabbis, and are not present on most of the lay decision-making bodies of the vast majority of denominations.

The question of ordination is a critical one: obviously the self-concept of a person (female) who needs a male link to the creator cannot be very high. Women are in the same position in the churches as we are elsewhere in society: just as male psychiatrists decide on the definition of our mental health, male priests interpret the Bible, which defines our spiritual condition.

The debate at the Women's Rights Convention (Seneca Falls, New York, 1854) included much on the woman's status in religion.[1]

> The Rev. Henry Grew, of Philadelphia, . . . felt it to be his duty to give his views on the questions under consideration. His opinions as to woman's rights and duties were based on the Scriptures. He quoted numerous texts to show that it was clearly the will of God that man should be superior in power and authority to woman; and asserted that no lesson is more plainly and frequently taught in the Bible, than woman's subjection.
>
> Mrs. Hannah Tracy Cutler of Illinois replied at length, and skillfully turned every text he had quoted directly against the reverend gentleman, to the great amusement of the audience. She showed that man and woman were a simultaneous creation, with equal power and glory on their heads, and that dominion over the fowl of the air, the fish of the sea, and every creeping thing on the earth was given to *them*, and not to man alone. The time has come for women to read and interpret Scripture for herself; too long have we learned God's will from the lips of man and closed our eyes on the great book of nature. . . . It is a pity that those who would recommend the Bible as the revealed will of the all-wise and benevolent Creator, should uniformly quote it on the side of tyranny and oppression.

In 1895 *The Woman's Bible*—a series of commentaries on those parts of the Bible that refer to women—caused an uproar within the suffragist movement, which was aspiring to respectability and feared alienating orthodox people who could be won to its cause. Elizabeth Cady Stanton insisted that women could achieve equality only when the pernicious influence of organized religion had been destroyed. *The Woman's Bible* gave fuel to those who claimed women were oppressed within the church.

> From the inauguration of the movement for woman's emancipation the Bible has been used to hold her in the "divinely ordained sphere," prescribed in the Old and New Testaments.
>
> The canon and civil law; church and state; priests and legislators; all political parties and religious demoninations have alike taught that woman was made after man, of man, and for man, an inferior being, subject to man. . . .
>
> The Bible teaches that women brought sin and death into the world, that she precipitated the fall of the race, that she was arraigned before the judgment seat of Heaven, tried, condemned and sentenced. Marriage was for her to be a condition of bondage, maternity a period of suffering and anguish, and in silence and subjection, she was to play the role of a dependent on man's bounty for all her material wants, and for all the information she might desire on the vital questions of the hour, she was commanded to ask her husband at home. Here is the Bible position of woman briefly summed up.

Chapter II, on Genesis II:21–25, explains the story of the creation of Eve from Adam's rib:

> There is something sublime in bringing order out of chaos, light out of darkness; giving each planet its place in the solar system; oceans and lands their limits; wholly inconsistent with a petty surgical operation, to find material for the mother of the race. It is on this allegory that all the enemies of woman rest their battering rams, to prove her inferiority.

Betty Bone Schiess,[2] who is attending the Seminary at Bexley Hall, Rochester, New York, and who hopes to be the first woman ordained as an Episcopal priest, said in a speech on February 14, 1970, in discussing the creation: "(Eve) was not made from Adam's brains because she might have done him in intellectually. She was not made from his foot; she might have crushed him."

The story of the creation of woman is degrading in many faiths. H. R. Hays[3] describes certain creation myths:

"Arab tradition provides us with some examples of the derogatory attitude. One group of Bedouins says that women were created from the sins of the satans, another that she was manufactured from the tail of a monkey. From the South Slavs we get other details; in this case God absentmindedly laid aside Adam's rib when he was performing the operation recorded in the Bible. A dog came along, snatched up the rib and ran off with it. God chased the thief but only succeeded in snatching off its tail. The best that could be done was to make a woman out of it. The Hebrews also made a contribution to the vilification of women with the daily prayer, 'I thank Thee, Lord, for not having created me a woman.' "

Dr. Hays connects the lowly interpretation of our creation with woman's being considered the source of all evil in the world. He suggests that the fall of man should rightly be called the fall of woman because once more the second sex is blamed for all the trouble in the world. Psychologically Pandora and Eve are parallel and even perhaps historically related, for it is pointed out: 'And Adam called his wife's name Eve; because she was the mother of all living,' a description with decided fertility goddess overtones. We are not told that Eve had a box, but she had a snake and an apple, which also have profound symbolic meanings.

In the Jewish religion, women are excluded from all public religious observances, from all active roles, although the Jewish woman does have many complicated rituals to perform in the home. One might say that she is so busy in the home that she barely has time to participate in the public life, even if she were so permitted. Ten persons are needed to pray in an Orthodox Jewish synagogue; they must be men. Women cannot say blessings on the altar. No women have been ordained as rabbis, although one[4] is currently studying to be a reformed Rabbi in Reformed Judaism. In orthodox Judaism, women sit in a balcony, separated from the men. The "cover story" for this is that their presence would distract the men from their work of praying. Actually, there is a strong taboo in orthodox Judaism against menstruating women: they are not allowed to touch food, or touch men. The separate seating insures against having to pray near a menstruating woman.

By allowing the woman to perform rituals in the house, and forbidding her to perform rituals in the temple, the religion effectively keeps woman in her place, and excludes her from public life.

In orthodox Judaism, people cannot get married on Saturday. This has been interpreted to mean that because a man cannot acquire property on Saturday, he cannot acquire a wife.* The husband can divorce the wife at will; the wife cannot get a divorce without the consent of the husband. Women have no *time-bound* commandments in the religion. This means that there is nothing specified for women to do at a particular time, such as praying. The rationale behind this is that such would interfere with her *primary* responsibility, which is the home and the children.

A boy enters the Jewish community at age thirteen, with a bar mitzvah. The feelings of a young girl, excluded from such entrance rites, are documented in the novel

---

*From conversation with Rabbi Richard A. Weiss, Congregation Kol Ami, Chicago, Illinois.

Marjorie Morningstar[5]:

> Preparations were underway for her brother Seth's bar mitzvah, scheduled for the Saturday before *The Mikado* performance. In Marjorie's view there was no comparing the importance of the two events. Her debut in the college show loomed as large in her mind as an opening night on Broadway; the bar mitzvah was a mere birthday party for a thirteen-year-old boy, with some religious frills. But obviously in the Morgenstern household nobody else thought as she did. Her parents seemed unaware that she was rehearsing at all. It astonished Marjorie to see how her mother's interest in her comings and goings dropped off. Even when she returned from dates with Sandy there were no eager question periods. . . . An unfamiliar sensation came over her at times—jealousy of Seth, of boys in general. Bar mitzvahs were not for girls. Her own birthday, which fell three weeks before Seth's, was going unmentioned.

This second-class citizenship of women was not altered with the advent of Christianity. Women are still considered, good for church (but not to run it), children, and kitchen. And, in addition, we are continually considered unclean.

St. Paul said: "It is good for a man not to touch a woman . . . but if they cannot contain, let them marry; for it is better to marry than to burn." Edward Westermarck connected the Paulist view of sexuality with uncleanliness. ". . . the defiling effects attributed to sexual intercourse are also no doubt connected with the notion that woman is an unclean being—regular temporary defilement of a specifically feminine character may easily lead to the notion of the permanent uncleanness of the female sex. And this is precisely what was achieved by Christian thinking."

A recent article in *Christian Century*[6] by Jeanne Richie well documents the systematic subordination of women in the church today:

Now and again voices are raised to remind us that the position of women in the church is something less than satisfactory. But this protest is easily ignored in the clamor about other problems. In this regard, the church pattern follows that which obtains in other areas of American life today. . . . [This] should be of particular concern to our churches, since they are so heavily dependent on the support of women and since few institutions so systematically deny women full participation.

Ms. Richie, after defining "caste" ("one of a series of hierarchically arranged ranks in a socially stratified system, . . . caste membership being by birth and not alterable during an individual's lifetime"), shows how women occupy a low caste in American society, and within the Christian church.

Men occupy the well-paid positions which give power and prestige, independence of action and control over resources; women do the ill-paid or unpaid work which is subordinate and supportive in nature. Women's work, whether in the home or outside, is characteristically monotonous, repetitive and confining. . . . nobody, neither men nor women, really wants to do about 99.9 per cent of what constitutes "women's work."

Most work settings in the United States are characterized by a division of labor based on sex. Typical is the secretary-businessman relationship. A recent article in *Newsweek* described more frankly than is the custom this division of labor and offers some intimations as to its destructive quality. Jack Nicklaus and F. Lee Bailey, are organizing Envoy International Town Clubs, Inc., "a haven away from home for the traveling executive." The clubs are equipped with attractive young women who will take dictation, fire off a letter, untangle snarled airline reservations, send telegrams and arrange conferences. In explaining the need for such services, Bailey says: "The thing that grinds you down traveling is doing the things a secretary normally does."

Although church membership and attendance are predominantly female, the lay boards which make church policy are largely male. . . . Church planners can count on the women to prepare refreshments for any function—and to clean up afterwards. A young woman who wants to make a career of religious work will find that about the only opening available to her is religious education, where she will always be in a subordinate and assisting relationship to the minister. There is no provision for her upward mobility into the ministry. For all practical purposes, the ministry is a caste system.

Ms. Richie explains the rigidity of "women's work," in the church and out of it.

If men are afraid of competition from women, they seem even more concerned lest women refuse one day to do the unpleasant jobs—which might then have to be done by men. So they play a sort of unending confidence game. They speak of housekeeping as "creative," even as "sacred." In their efforts to keep women confined to drudgery, they sometimes become almost coercive . . . in other words, . . . men have available to them a noncritical, noncompetitive servant-caste, people who not only carry out orders rapidly and efficiently but also with flattery and charm.

In recent years churches have acknowledged their obligation to support the campaign of black Americans for full rights. There is little comparable concern for women's rights. As Ms. Richie says, "When (clergymen) urge their white congregations to become more active in assisting minority groups, they are in effect asking one disadvantaged group to help another disadvantaged group—asking women to abandon their own struggle and devote their energies to helping a group that is not much worse off than the women themselves."

Betty Bone Schiess agrees[7]: "In working within the church, I found that women are more discriminated against than blacks." Her own crusade for ordination grew out of her long time involvement in the fight to obtain rights for black people in the Episcopal church.

Ms. Richie concludes: "Of the people who are active

in the church, the majority are women. But this remnant can be driven out of the church, if they continue to be invisible to ministers and if they are forced to remain the subordinate group in a sex-caste system."

Persons deeply concerned with the church as a moral force consider the sex-caste system of sex discrimination more shocking there than in other institution of society. Elsie Thomas Culver[8] comments:

> The double standards of responsibility, expectations, and pay for church work as between men and women are really shocking anachronisms of which the secular world is well aware; they lower the respect for religion in the eyes of the government bureau, the honest businessman, or the union member. It is often said that the women going into church work as a professional career needs to be told that she had better be at the top of her class (which she frequently is), work twice as hard, twice as many hours, and demand only half the pay and none of the credit, if she is to succeed.

Women in the United States are known to be "more religious" than men. Gordon Allport[9] found that women "make up a larger proportion of church membership, take a larger part in religious-group affairs, and express more interest in religion when asked about their beliefs than men do. . . . 82% of the women students reported need for a religious orientation as compared with 76% of non-veteran men and 64% of veterans."

In a sample of native-born Protestants in Indianapolis, Lenski[10] found a highly significant difference in the extent of religious interest between men and women. A third of the men expressed "little" interest, but only 20% of the men indicated "much" interest, compared with over 38% of the women.

More interesting than these figures is an explanation of why women are more church-minded, despite the fact that they can achieve little power in the church. J. Milton

Yinger, professor of Sociology and Anthropology at Oberlin College, writes:[11] "The rights and duties embodied in their role expectations in American society give them less latitude and choice. They are expected to abide more closely by the traditional standards of the culture than are men. . . . Women in general have narrower contacts and have therefore experienced somewhat less secularization than men." The tensions inherent in a situation where there is "an equalitarian ideology but many non-equalitarian facts" has created what Yinger aptly calls "some 'minority group' influences" on female religious behavior.

Perhaps one of the attractions of the church for women is the seductiveness of any organization or institution that promises "pie in the sky." When your hopes, dreams, and aspirations are not fulfilled on earth, you are much more inclined to be attracted to a dogma that gives promise of better things in the life to come. And, to be very practical, when you have few places in the outer world which are open to you, and from which you can derive social gratification, you may indeed go to church.

Another connection between women and the church stems from the similarity between the value systems of the church and the family. L. F. Wood suggests:[12] "The church has its roots in the family values. Witness such ideas as God our Father, love as the heart of religion, the brotherhood of man as a philosophy of social living, the bearing of one another's burdens, the forgiveness of offenses, doing to others as we would have them do to us, and sacrificial love as the means of helping those who most need help."

In addition to playing a major role in birth, marriage, and death, the church sustains the patriarchial tradition by setting standards for sexual conduct, family planning, and the education of the young. Family life is frequently a topic for sermons.

The family that prays together stays together. And, in addition, priests, rabbis, and ministers give family counseling and may indeed set the standards for secular family counseling.

In *Bed and Board: Plain Talk About Marriage*,[13] The Very Reverend Robert Farrar Capon gives advice. He, "his wife and their six children live—amidst sea breezes, ensemble music, and the aromas of Mrs. Capon's wonderful cooking—in a rambling old house in Port Jefferson, New York, where Father Capon has been, since 1949, Vicar of Christ Church (Episcopal)," as the dust jacket notes.

Father Capon explains sex differences: "The truth of our being is that we are one species, but just barely. Even without counting porpoises, this planet houses two different sorts of rationality, two different kinds of freedom, and two different brands of love: men's and women's. . . . The abstractness of the male intellect, the concreteness of the female, the man's characteristic grasp of the whole and the woman's typical attention to the part, his minding of the bank balance and hers to the children's need for underwear."

It is difficult enough, for a woman whose marriage counselor or psychiatrist tells her that her intellect is best used in determining the children's need for underwear, to say this is crazy—that the advice-giver is crazy. But when it comes from a man of God, the woman is in deeper trouble: she has more difficulty rejecting the "advice."

Father Capon explains the Paulist attitude to marriage.

> St. Paul may [sic] have been prejudiced toward women [what with not letting them speak in church]. . . . The husband, he says, is the head of the wife, just as Christ is the head of the Church. The marriage rite takes him at his word. It is the groom who speaks first. . . . The bride is to obey, to receive and to respond. . . . The Bible does

not say that *men* and *women* are unequal. . . . It is the *husbands* and *wives* that are unequal. It is precisely in marriage (a state, you will recall, not to be continued as such in heaven) that they enter into a relationship of superior to inferior—of head to body. . . . The husband is over his wife as the head is over the body. It isn't a description of what ought to be; it just says what *is*. He *is* the head. . . . If he doesn't initiate, she will wither of neglect. She cannot supply what only he can give.

Later he notes, "As a priest, I listen dutifully to a lot of wifely discontent. Women have their faults, and I don't suppose there is a pastor on earth who doesn't at times wish he had the power to convert them all back into ribs—nice, quiet, uncomplaining ribs."

Despite this condescending attitude toward women, Father Capon *understands* the inevitability of our function. In a section on modern conveniences, he says: "Though she bakes packaged mixes, she still bakes; though she no longer spins and weaves, she still clothes and mends; though she is surrounded by machinery to do her work, she herself still moves in the old orbit: from sink to stove to store, and round and round again. And all this is a great mercy. Her function forces itself upon her."

The "mercy" in our preordained future is apparent even when we go to work. "Women go to work; sometimes simply to find fulfillment, sometimes on the basis of real necessity; but often only to get more money to buy more devices to spare themselves for more work. Yet in few cases do they work at anything worth saving themselves for. They plough through their motherly functions every day—most of them do fabulously well; they are a remarkable breed—but then they escape for fulfillment to some bit of a ten-to-four clerking or six-to-twelve piecework that is less fulfilling than making instant chocolate pudding. The really dreadful part of it all is the wear and tear; for by definition, and by choice, they are not substituting one function for another, but acting two roles on the strength of only one small heart."

Father Capon makes some practical suggestions.

> Don't burn the kneading trough yet. As a working mother, or a mother with a career, you certainly won't use it often. But remember, you are a landmark.
>
> Dispose yourself to be loved, to be wanted, to be available. Be *there* for them with a vengeance. Be a gracious, bending women. Incline your ear, your heart, your hands to them . . . Be ready to be done by and to welcome their casual effusions with something better than preoccupation and indifference.
>
> I think the use of contraceptive devices is ridiculous, not so much on the basis of unnaturalness as on the basis of love and the dance. Between the devices and the pills, it becomes a ballet conducted via an assortment of blocks and tackles, of jibs, booms and rigging. There is just too much fuss over equipment, and too many coy but urgent little trips. On the other hand, the so-called rhythm system is not much better. While it allows the ballet to go on without all that rigging, it doesn't allow it to go on with much spontaneity.

And, if you let the love and the dance go on without contraception, and you don't like all the results, it is *your* fault, lady.

"The wives who feel trapped may have chiefly themselves to blame. They will not or cannot accept the realities of marriage: that it is part of a wife's bargain to maintain her home, to care for her children, and to be a helpmate in every sense of the word."[14]

Similar guidance is dispensed by Charles W. Shedd, also a minister.[15]

". . . one of my first bits of advice on how to treat a woman is 'take charge!' For the good of your marriage, for the good of your children-to-be, and for the good of the nation's future I hope you'll read me loud and clear

. . . don't forget that the kind of authority we're talking about here is the authority of love. It seems to me that nearly every woman I know wants a man who knows how to love, with authority!"

Dr. Shedd explains how to convince your wife that you value her for things other than sexual pleasure: tell her about how grand are her other skills.

> The surest safeguard, obviously, is to praise her biscuits and her housekeeping; how well she manages your money; how nice she looked at the party; the new apron she made; and anything else you like about her. . . . Note how these center on a man's assurance that he is being satisfied. This is terribly important to a woman. Not only does she want to feel that she is fulfilling the basic female function of pleasing her mate, but she loves to know that he will be carrying lovely memories to feed back into his thoughts.

The church's sanctification of the slave role of women is *implied* by all these definitions of how the basic female role is to please her mate, but it is *demonstrated* by examining the actual role of women in the church. The World Council of Churches surveyed the status of women's ordination in 1963, and these statistics have been informally updated since. The Roman Catholic church does not ordain women priests. No women are allowed to be rabbis, in the orthodox, conservative, or reform branches of Judaism. The Greek Orthodox and related eastern churches do not ordain women. Only one woman has been ordained in an Anglican church. This was in China, when there was a desperate wartime shortage of men priests. This action was later deplored by the Lambeth Conference as a "most unwelcome unilateral act." The Lutheran church, which with the Episcopalians was the last stronghold of not ordaining women in the Protestant church, has just (June 1970) voted to admit women to the ministry. The convention voted to change the word "man" in the qualifications for ordination, to "person."

The study commission, which had presented the recommendation to the convention, stated that "the crux of the matter is justice."

The Methodist church has ordained women for some time, but with no assurance of appointment. In 1956 it gave women full clergy rights. The Baptists ordain women, as does the Congregational church. The United Presbyterian church in America has ordained women since 1956. The Salvation Army runs on the basis of "full" equality—except that a wife cannot earn more money or hold a higher rank than her husband in the Army!

As mentioned earlier, the Episcopal church does not ordain women as priests. In May 1970, women delegates to the annual meeting of the American Baptist Convention served notice that next year they will demand a woman president. Women have been given the right to read the Bible and to act as song leaders during Catholic mass, when no men are available. The Vatican, however, recently refused to accredit a woman diplomat as West Germany's representative at the Vatican.

Women in the church are beginning to rebel. The National Coalition of American Nuns, representing 1,500 sisters, issued a statement in July 1969, saying: "We protest any domination of our institution by priests, no matter what their hierarchial status."

The subordinate role of women in the church is both a reflection of, and an example to, the rest of the society. The genesis of the discrimination to women in religion is often explained by her role in creation. Thus, Krister Stendahl[16] states: "In all of the texts where the New Testament speaks about the role of women in the church, we have found that when a reason is given, it is always by reference to the subordinate position of women in the order of creation. This applies to her place in the home, in society, and even in the church, *i.e.*, when she is 'in Christ.' "

On Independence Day 1970, the General Assembly of the Unitarian Universalist Association passed a sweeping resolution calling for equal rights and opportunities for women. It asked for "special efforts within the church to utilize women in important positions, including the ministry." At this time, there are 10 women and 874 men in the ministry of the Unitarian Universalist church.

Dr. Stendahl posits the only logical position which all churches can take: "The only alternative . . . is to recognize the legal, economic, political, and professional emancipation of women, and that with joy and gratitude, as a great achievement. . . . If emancipation is right, then there is no valid 'biblical' reason not to ordain women."

NOTES TO CHAPTER IV

1. Quoted in *Up From the Pedestal: Selected Writings in the HIstory of American Feminism*, edited by Aileen S. Kraditor, Chicago: Quadrangle Books, 1968.
2. On October 17, 1970, the House of Deputies of the Episcopal Church defeated a motion to permit the ordination of women to the priesthood and the episcopacy. The *New York Times*, October 18, reports: "Those opposed to the move expressed fear that an ordained female clergy would increasingly prejudice friendly Episcopal relations with the Roman Catholic and Eastern Orthodox churches. Neither of these communions permits the ordination of women. . . . One priest made the point that there were no women among the apostles. The negative vote of the deputies came only three days after the women of the church, meeting also in Houston, Texas, in triennial session, voted 222 to 45 in favor of female ordination." The matter will be brought up again in 1973.
3. Hays, H. R., *The Dangerous Sex*: The Myth of Feminine Evil, New York: G. P. Putnam's Sons, 1964, p. 12.
4. Sally Priesand is in her fourth year at Cincinnati's Hebrew Union College.
5. Wouk, Herman, *Marjorie Morningstar*, Garden City, New Jersey: Doubleday & Company, Inc., 1955.
6. Richie, Jeanne, *Christian Century*, "Church, Caste, and Women," January 21, 1970, pp. 73–77.
7. Quoted in *Christian Century*, January 21, 1970, p. 72.
8. Culver, Elsie Thomas, *Women in the World of Religion*, Garden City, New York: Doubleday & Company, Inc., 1967, p. 285.
9. Allport, Gordon, *The Individual and His Religion*, p. 37.
10. Lenski, Gerhard, "Social Correlates of Religious Interest," *American Sociological Review*, October 1953, pp. 535–36.
11. Yinger, J. Milton, *Religion, Society and the Individual*, New York: The Macmillan Company, 1957, p. 93.
12. Wood, L. F., "Church Problems in Marriage Education," *The Annals of the American Academy of Political and Social Science*, 272, November 1950, p. 177.
13. Capon, Robert Farrar, *Bed and Board: Plain Talk About Marriage*, New York: Simon and Schuster, 1965.
14. Norman Lobsenz and Clark Blackburn, *How to Stay Married*, a Family Service Association of America publication.
15. Shedd, Charles W., *Letters to Philip: On How to Treat a Woman*, Old Tappan, New Jersey: Spire Books, 1968.
16. Stendahl, Krister. *The Bible and the Role of Woman*: A Case Study of Hermeneutics, Philadelphia, Pa.: Fortress Press, 1966, p. 38–39.

CHAPTER V

Home and Family Life:
What you Learn at Home
about Being a Woman

*T*HE FIRST THING that a girl learns in her family is that Daddy is King. This learning only takes place in the normal, healthy family. If she comes from a broken home, she doesn't learn this so young, unless of course the father has left the family without money, in which case the lesson is learned through negative implication.

If she has brothers, she quickly learns that they are preparing to be daddies (kings). A psychoanalytic explanation of family interaction is: the mother loves her sons; the daughter is jealous of this love; the daughter is also jealous of the fact that Daddy loves Mommy (sexually) and not her; the daughter wants love from Daddy and thinks that when she grows up she will be a woman and hence attract love from a man, perhaps not quite as good as Daddy, but pretty good anyway. Another explanation of mother-daughter problems is that the daughter resents her mother's being "castrated," and therefore considers the mother responsible for own "castration." She then rejects the mother as a love-object and turns to the father.

If one accepts the idea that the goal of every child is to mate with the parent of the opposite sex, the above makes sense. I submit a much more logical analysis: It is obvious that Daddy rules the house. It is obvious that Mommy is breaking her back trying to please him. A female child knows she will grow up to be a Mommy. She must learn to please Daddy. The key to *power* in the house is via the father. So, one must cozy up to power. Would a "normal" person aspire to serve dinner, or to be served dinner? The answer is apparent.

Elizabeth Koontz, director of the Labor Department's Women's Bureau, told the Women's National Democratic Club[1] that the nation is deprived of female brainpower, which is very harmful to the nation and to the females. She discussed the "southern belle" syndrome which "conditions us as women to be reared in a cocoon of thinking. An 'SB' is taught to praise Papa for being good to her and providing for her well-being, in return for which she must kiss and flatter him and never question his judgments. She carries this habit through courtship, and ultimately is a full-fledged SB—dependent, non-aggressive and rumored to be brainless."

The southern belle syndrome is not limited to the South. Moreover, in so-called enlightened families of to-day, the kinds of dependency which are scorned in chil-dren—both male and female—are encouraged in grown women. Young girls are encouraged to earn their own money; a parent beams with pride when daughter starts up a baby-sitting business. This typically in middle-class families is not because they need the money, but because the attempt at financial independence shows a striving for automony that parents respect in children. Yet, the wife who is supported for twenty-five years by her husband is not considered dependent; she is considered normal and proper.

Although many parents "pry" into the lives of their children, most of them admire a child who does her/his own thing, makes plans without consulting them, has independent ideas and executes them into action. This is encouraged because it is a sign of health, a sign of *growing up*. Even the so-called neurotic parent is distressed when the child asks instructions every step of the way in growing up. Not so with the wife. The typical husband encourages dependence, not only economic, but psychological. We all know from our experience that if Mommy comes up with some plan all on her own, without consulting Daddy, and executes it, he will not like it. He feels left out. Husbands are jealous, not usually of actual male lovers of their wives, but of the *real* lovers: outside interests. Women are teased mercilessly about their pursuits: garden club, bridge games, art gallery browsing. Ostensibly this is because these activities are not as significant as what the husband is doing: making money in the world of the male.

The daughter observing this teasing of Mother and her pursuits first assumes that window-shopping "with the girls" is silly and that is why Daddy is making fun of it. This naturally causes confusion in the daughter, who doesn't know exactly what she will do when she grows up. She is female, so she will be like Mother. And then, the power figure (Daddy) will tease her about her activities, whereas now both Mother and Father are praising her for good grades, leadership qualities, and her imagination.

However, when this process is analyzed it turns out to be something more than it first seemed. When Mother is pursuing activities *more* significant than the weekly card game the problems really start. When Mother says: you all tend to your clothes and food needs and chauffeuring tasks now, I am going to medical school to be a doctor—then the family crisis really begins.

How do we know that Daddy is King? First of all, there is the service. Some men "help with the dishes," but when everyone is being honest it is clear who buys the food, who cooks it, who cleans up afterward, who buys the clothes, who mends them, who washes them (and who gets very upset when they don't come out of the machine with colors brighter than bright). Mother does all this. If the family has money, Mother instructs someone else to do it. Very few men will even talk to household help. This phenomenon derives from their view that household work is women's work. If they, with all their education and high income, can afford household help, at least they do not have to direct these menial activities.

There is a politics of housework that every young woman should be aware of. The same oppressions which condition a young female not to aspire to high-paying jobs, the same society which makes difficult her entrance into educational programs and into jobs where she could in fact earn a high income (should she, despite societal messages decide to go into a "man's" occupation), condition both men and women to think that personal service is for women to perform. Just as the black slave in the South "took care of the family," the female takes care of the family.

I have observed that married feminists, when interviewed on television, frequently say that everything in their house is equal: they share the household chores and the child-rearing tasks. They are equals. I have no doubt that this is sometimes true. But usually it is not. I personally have never known a man who did his share of taking care of *himself*. Men who have cooked and cleaned while unmarried, cease this activity the minute they live with a woman, whether she be lover or wife. They then "help her with the shopping." This is a reality which has nothing to do with biology: it is a political reality that every woman must learn. Men divide nicely into two categories via à vis domestic chores. Most men consider this junk a female domain, and have nothing to do with it, in thought or in action. Some men, who do know how to cook, or who have views on child-raising, play the role of critic. They, because they are men, can do everything better, and they tell this in no uncertain terms to the female who is frying the potatoes: "you are frying those potatoes wrong."

Women cannot stop frying the potatoes—yet. We have no money, we need someone to buy the potatoes or we will starve. Women are supported by husbands, by fathers, by lovers, or (poorly supported) by the welfare departments (run by men). So, in 1970, we either cook for the men, or we don't eat. In 1980 the situation will be different.

A young girl learns first that Daddy is King because of the service he gets. Secondly, she learns he is King because the whole family is dependent on him for food. Mother and children are (naturally) grateful to him for providing this money so they can live. A typical remark in middle-class families is "I slave away all day in the law office so you can live in this gorgeous house in the suburbs." This is supposed to elicit gratefulness. Even children's textbooks contain such dogma: The following is from a third grade social studies book,[2] written to teach eight-year-old children about life, in this case life in the suburbs and why the family lives there.

> "Sometimes I wish I did work here," said Dad. "But my work is in the city. You know that I am an engineer. The company I work for builds bridges and big buildings. I work in their office, so that means I must commute. A

commuter is a person who travels back and forth every day between his home in the suburbs and his job in a big city."

"Couldn't we live in San Francisco?" asked Ted. "Then you wouldn't have to commute. We could all be together more often."

"When you were just a little boy, we did live there," said Father. "We liked living in the city. I went to work by streetcar or bus. But we moved to the suburbs because we wanted more room for you children to play in. Now we have a larger house and a bigger yard."

"Mother likes to grow pretty flowers in the yard. Here in the suburbs we have enough room for Mother to grow almost anything. But I do have to take a train to work every day."

As Betty Friedan so vividly first pointed out in 1963, the suburbs are the final prison for women. Whereas a woman who lives in the city can at least *get out* and see the world, the woman in the suburbs is there, all day.

A recent article in the *Ladies Home Journal* dispensed well with the myth of the wonderful time women have in the suburbs. The author said that the husbands in her New Jersey community are high-paid ($60,000 a year) executives and travel much of the time. When they come home, they are exhausted, either from twenty meetings in twenty-four hours or twenty parties in twenty-four hours. The women are in effect abandoned for much of the week because of the travel schedules of the husbands. When the husbands are "at home," they are out playing golf or tennis. She said that the community is totally devoid of men over age twelve most of the time. The myth that the suburbs are a hotbed of sexual intrigue is not correct: there are no men there with whom to intrigue. The women find solace in drinking, and are for the most part very depressed.

The implications of this statement for women's liberation are enormous. The solution is not, of course, to force executive husbands to spend more time at the barbeque pit. Perhaps their absence is a good message. They are saying that it is dull at home in the suburbs. The excitement is out in the world, and those who can determine where they are (the men), choose not to be in the home. But more significant is the fact that the women (most of whom have college educations and enough money to hire help for child care and house cleaning) have nothing to do! Needless to say, if they were as busy with their careers as their husbands are, they would not be frustrated. Any mentally and physically competent adult who sits in a large expensive mansion waiting for another adult to come home and bring in the outer world deserves sympathy, certainly, but mostly a mandate to reexamine her life.

The lesson from the social studies textbook, which is typical of the kinds of family life learning which children get in school, is a classic example of male-dominant society dogma permeating the primary grades. We are to assume that Daddy, at great sacrifice to himself (he must ride the train) moved out to the suburbs so the children could play in the yard and Mother could grow flowers. There is no mention of how men enjoy living in the suburbs: a large country house is a status symbol; often it is convenient for men to have their work and their homes separated by some miles.

But the really dangerous message here is not that poor Daddy makes sacrifices for the family. It is the message to eight-year old boys and girls that when they grow up the boys will build bridges and big buildings, and the girls will sit out in the country and grow flowers.

Another important myth about family living which must be exploded is that of an identity between female maturity and liking housework. According to a prevalent attitude, it is the immature girl who enjoys only her honeymoon, with all its romance and sandy beaches, and then comes back to her small newlywed's apartment and collapses at the realization that it is *she* who will have to do shopping, cooking, cleaning, washing, and ironing. If she is "grown up" (well trained by her mother and her schooling) she is supposed to dive with relish into these tasks, and spend her spare time thinking up how to do them better: don't broil a hamburger for dinner, make meatloaf à la Pouffe for the man in your life.

This slave psychology must be ended once and for all. No human being will naturally (no matter how lovely the gift roses, no matter how exciting the love-making) want to shop, cook, clean, wash, and iron. These are basically unpleasant tasks, and only the most effective brainwash in the world could make anyone want to do them. This most effective brainwash in the world has indeed taken place, as can be observed by reading any woman's magazine, or sadder yet, observing highly educated and intelligent women, who go to these slave tasks with relish, making them bearable only by elaborating on them.

Dr. Alan Porter, a family doctor writing in the *British Medical Journal*,[3] reports that wives are sixty times more likely to become depressed than single women. Dr. Porter spent three years studying depression among his patients. In that time he found that of ninety-two patients who complained about depression, only one was a single woman. Fourteen complainers were men, twelve of whom were married. The others consisted of sixty-seven married women, six widows, and four divorcees. "Married women," the doctor concludes, "are prone to the disorder at any time in their lives and relapse is frequent."

The family is the prototype for oppression. The superiority and importance of the father, despite his actual capacity and skills, is the prototype for the oppression of the poor by the rich, the black by the white, and the young by the old.

Engels[4] explained that the division of labor in our early history was that men took care of the cattle and women did the farming as well as raising children and doing the domestic chores. They were considered equal occupations, each necessary and each contributing to the good of the community. Then came the concept of trading, and cattle became the ultimate unit of exchange. Since men were responsible for the cattle, they became the first property owners. Since the property could not be passed on to sons if paternity was uncertain, sexual pairing became necessary, along with strict fidelity. Soon women, like cattle, became the property of men.

The family unit today is where sex roles are learned, where the superiority of men is made clear. So important is this function considered to the society in general, that in literature on "broken homes," it is usually stressed that one of the so-called "tragedies" of the broken home is that the children have trouble learning their proper sex roles.

The family is also the institution which, through the emphasis on home, aids in keeping women from running the city. This is strengthened by the lack of community provision of "home functions," such as food processing centers and child care facilities.

William O'Neill[5] explains the failure of the early suffrage movement in America. Women got the vote after a century of fighting for it, and then proceeded to elect men to public office for the next fifty years. He says he, as a "scholar," is avoiding the question of whether or not women *ought* to have full parity with men. However, he argues "that it was a mistake (though probably an unavoidable one) for Victorian feminists to abandon their critique of marriage, not because I am in favor of free love but because it seems evident that the institutions of marriage and the family, as presently conceived, are among the chief obstacles to feminine equality."

Ronald V. Sampson[6] describes Victorian society, and its lessons about liberty and power. "The Victorian family as depicted by Samuel Butler is essentially an unholy alliance between an overbearing but petty patriarch and a vain adulatory consort for the purpose of deceiving their offspring as to the real nature of their parents and of a society composed of them and their like."

Until "the father as the unmistakable head of the household" concept is undone, women will always run the house for men, and never run the city.

NOTES TO CHAPTER V

1. Quoted in *Miami Herald,* May 1970.
2. *We Look Around Us,* Hunnicutt, *et al,* L. W. Singer, 1963, p. 63.
3. Quoted in *Parade* Magazine, May 17, 1970.
4. Engels, Friedrich. *The Origins of the Family, Private Property and the State* (1884). Translated by Ernest Untermann, Chicago: Charles Kerr, 1902.
5. O'Neill, William, *Everyone Was Brave: The Rise and Fall of Feminism in America,* Chicago: Quadrangle Books, 1969.
6. Sampson, Ronald V., *The Psychology of Power,* New York: Pantheon Books, 1966, p. 104.

CHAPTER VI

Mother

ONE OF the most dangerous myths around is that every red-blooded American girl is supposed to hate her mother. It is dangerous because it further separates woman from woman (female solidarity and self-interest should override even the generation gap). It is a myth because it is not true. The reason for most of the mother-daughter hatred which does exist is not that they are competing for the love of the father; it is not the generation gap; it *is* that the mother is the tool by which society socializes the daughter into the role of woman.

In other words, it is your mother who must give you the message loud and clear: you are here to please men; you must please men to survive; you must sublimate your own aspirations and desires to accomplish this—*as she did.* And she didn't enjoy doing it. Even in the most domestic and *Ladies Home Journal*-model-wife-and-mother, there lurks a rage. She doesn't like being everyone's servant, and she certainly doesn't like the job of training her beloved daughter for the same fate.

She has little alternative than to do this. No mother

wants to raise a misfit, and any mother who doesn't in-
doctrinate her young girls with the mystique of the beauty
of second-class citizenship, knows she will have a misfit
on her hands. And worse yet, she will have a daughter
who never marries, thereby making the family a failure
because they did not raise a successful daughter (woman's
success is always measured by the quality of the husband
she marries).

Mothers are often miserable that they have caused so
much resentment on the part of their daughters. What
they fail to realize is that they have been tragically and
often unknowingly a part of the conspiracy to keep women
in their place. Not only must the mother reinforce so-
called feminine traits in her daughter, but often the only
reinforcement given the child by the father is praise for
being coy, cute, sexy, flirty. In this way, the daughter is
further driven to personally destructive behavior, in order
to win *anyone's* approval.

In addition to being the "foreman" of the sex-role
system, the mother of the family has an additional problem which creates rage in herself: she doesn't have any
money. There is an old cliché: he who pays the piper
calls the tune. Women are encouraged—from the days
when they were young girls being told not to prepare
themselves for a career because they would some day
"get married," to the day they have a child and the whole
world tells them to stay home and tend it or risk being
called a poor mother—not to earn money or even to be
equipped to earn money.

Shirley Chisholm said[1]: "Women cannot, for the most
part, operate independently of men because they often
do not have sufficient economic freedom." What this
means to our mothers is that, denied both the training
and opportunity to develop their own talents and *to make*

money, they are dependent for food for themselves and their children upon a man. Moreover, they are not in this position because of "outside jailers" alone. The slave in the South at least knew he was being held in bondage and didn't think he was on the plantation because he loved it. Our mothers place themselves in this position because of "love."

When one cannot express discontent (over being totally economically dependent on another person who may or *may not* have your self-interest at heart), one feels rage. The average mother sees very little of the outside world, so her rage turns to her children, to her husband. Most of it stays in herself.

The bitchy woman, the clutching mother, the nagging wife are such stereotypes in our literature and in the mass media that it is unnecessary to define them. Needless to say, I would not be naive enough to say that if women were liberated there would be nothing but peace and harmony in the family situation. (The closeness and lack of autonomy and privacy in family living will always cause problems.) However, I would go so far as to say that if women were not consistently frustrated in achieving their own aims, they would not be so bitchy. If wives did not feel that their husbands were out in the world, working with ideas and meeting interesting people, while they were washing dishes and chauffeuring the kids—they would not nag.

Women *are* jealous of men, wives of their husbands. This has nothing to do with penis envy. Your mother is jealous of your father because he is developing himself, year after year, as a person, and she is not. She is, in fact, gaining lesser status as the years go on. When a baby is small, it needs constant care, and will die if left alone. Therefore, the mother who spends full time caring for it is an *important* person. As a child grows older, it needs less care. The role of the mother becomes extraneous; she is less important.

"Having been increasingly exposed to people more socially and intellectually developed than he, [the husband] becomes polished, while [the wife] remains more or less the same. I think it not unfair to say that in America, one can tell how far a man has risen by meeting his wife—that is, his first wife."[2]

The wife's jealousy of her husband is not concealed. Ads for airplane companies and restaurants and credit cards say: Don't leave her at home. Take her along. Don't have all this fun while she stays at home with the children. The clear message is that women *are* left out of a lot of fun in the world, and that they resent it.

Since the average American woman has her youngest child in full-time school by the time she is thirty-two years old, we are in effect retiring women at age thirty-two. The various anxieties that beset men at age sixty-five when they retire from their work (and increasingly, mandatory retirement is being reexamined because of the problems it causes for the individual), come to the woman at age thirty-two. Since people of thirty-two are much more vigorous and healthy, it is obvious that being forcefully retired causes more anxiety in the woman. Evidence of this anxiety and depression is seen in the alcoholism rates for women, the great number of women going to psychiatrists, and the huge number who have unnecessary surgery—all in the hope of alleviating their empty and "sick" feelings.

When the man retires, if he had a position of importance, he is often encouraged to continue on as a consultant. Although his replacements may or may not welcome his suggestions, we can assume they file them in the wastebasket if the ideas are not functional. At the very least, we know that the authors of the country are not busy writing novels telling about how retired men are ruining American business and the professions. We know that comedians cannot get an instant laugh by telling an anecdote about a retired man trying to keep his hand in his old job. We know that all problems which beset the employment situation after his retirement are not *automatically* blamed on him.

Not so fortunate is the mother. She has been trained from early childhood to play with dolls, to aspire to motherhood as her most important, her only, significant goal. For a few years—during pregnancy, while the children are pre-school—she is adulated by the mass media, by the advertisers. People give her a seat on the bus and coo at the baby. In six years, she is finished. Not only is the majority of her work finished (the cooking and cleaning continues for life—the child-raising is taken over for the most part by the school and the community), she is *punished severely* for trying to keep working. Every contemporary novel has a Sophie Portnoy for us to scorn. Men and children are busy telling mother to keep her hands off the children. Everything bad that happens—the child shoots dope, the child flunks out of school, the child cracks up the car—is automatically the mother's fault. Typically it is her fault because she didn't raise the child properly. Often it is her fault because she smothered him/her with too much of that motherly over-solicitude.

As long as motherhood is *the* occupation for women, mothers will continue venting their rage on their families. Mothers will continue prying into the lives of their husbands and children: they don't have their own lives.

Many people, particularly young women, are acutely uncomfortable around their mothers. This is because daughters are, consciously or unconsciously, aware of the gross unfairness of the life situation of the mother. Young women, filled with the normal ego drives of any healthy person, can see that mother has been conditioned to "live for others," and this makes the "others" feel uncomfortable.

The guilt of children probably does not stem from wishing the death of the parents, as psychoanalysts tell us. The guilt, at least toward the mother, would naturally stem from watching another human being submerge all the pleasures and delights of self, of doing your own thing. Whether the mother develops into the bitch or the martyr ("I gave my life for you and what do I get back?"), the origin of the problem is the same: she has *in fact* given up her life and is fully entitled to be furious about it.

In spring 1970, I spoke in Detroit, Michigan, and received the usual bunch of letters following a newspaper account of what I said. One letter illustrates perfectly the success of the brainwash women are submitted to.

> I prepare meals and clean up afterwards because I love the people for whom I cook and like to see them well fed. I wash and iron articles of clothing and linens because I love the people who use them. I clean house because I like the house which is mine to clean and I love the people who live here. I enjoy living in a clean home myself and like the people I love to have a clean home in which to live. . . . I accepted my husband's proposal of marriage because I love him. He did not force me to marry him. When I accepted his proposal I knew what he expected of me.

When a man loves and is loved, his "job" is to develop himself and go out into the city. When a child loves and is loved, his or her job is to develop and do well and achieve. When a woman, your mother, loves and is loved, her job is to iron the linens.

We all scorn the woman who brags about her children. Showing off one's home with its expensive gadgets is in poor taste. Women are ridiculed for being clotheshorses, for bragging about their great apple pie. This double whammy shows just how bad things are. Your mother is relegated to raising you, to cleaning the house. Women as a political class must be proud of the children and the house. That is their domain. If they show off anything else (a woman self-confidently talking at a party about her profession), the whole world mourns the neglected children and the dusty house.

The final humiliation about women's work—church, children, and kitchen—is that women do not run these spheres in the world. The church is run exclusively by men, many denominations not even allowing women to be ordained, or to lead prayers. The best cooks are men, everyone knows that. A woman speaking about sex differences told the audience that men, being more creative, are not cookbook cooks, but rather use their special imaginations to invent recipes. The heads of the interior decorating profession are men. Architects who design the houses in which we spend our lives are men; women have practically an impossible time either getting into architecture school or in getting a decent job after they have graduated, should they have been lucky enough to get into school.

The give away about women's status is, however, men's relationship to child-raising. It may be said that cooking and cleaning are dull and unimportant, but it is agreed by all that the raising of children is a (perhaps the) prime function of the society. This is why men are the experts on child-raising.

The child psychology experts have been men: Dr. Gessell, Angelo Patri, and finally, Dr. Spock. It is a man like Dr. Spock, who lives a fulfilling professional and political life, who tells the women of America that their children will develop best if Mama stays at home. It is Dr. Spock who tells the women of America that they shouldn't work unless it is absolutely necessary for the money.

One of the firmest indications of the lack of self-love of women in this period is that we *listen* to these expert men who tell us how to run our lives. If there has been one domain which was the woman's, it has been bringing up children. No one could claim being in the house all day is a very effective way to live, but at least it was one's domain. The myth that men do everything better has now seeped down to raising the baby.

The first director of the newly-formed Office of Child Development, an agency in the Department of Health, Education and Welfare, is a man, Dr. Edward Frank Zigler. "My politics are children," he said.[3]

Although women have not made any headway in getting into "men's" fields, men have done very well in women's fields. Library science, education, and social work—formerly the domain of women—have now attracted men to their training programs. As a result, the men hold the administrative positions both in the institutions of higher education and in the field. Also, these professions now have higher status, and higher pay. The field of child development is also attracting men. Many self-hating female educators welcome this with incredible remarks about how children need the good influence of men.

A recent article, describing an experimental nursery school in New York, which uses the latest methods for the cognitive and affective development of children, had a series of pictures in a weekly magazine. The photos showed young men (only) playing with the children. The caption gave the explanation: the reason there were *men* playing with the children is that this is a special nursery school and uses very intellectual and sophisticated methods. We are to assume if it were an ordinary crackers-and-milk nursery school it would be staffed by women.

Your mother must, as an agent of the society, help you as a young girl with two principal problems, from which the male is largely exempt.[4] "One is that of renunciation. [The young girl] must understand, accept, acquiesce to or rebel against the dictates of society which relegate her to second class status. She must deal with the reality which tells her that anatomy is destiny—that she must indeed do the dishes and become the mistress of the menial only because she has a uterus. Excluded from the definitive and consequential affairs in the community in which she must live, she must come to accept that her role is to be one of passivity and submission.

"Secondly is the problem of sexual infidelity on the part of the parents. . . . not errant sexual behavior of the parents but of the turning away from the daughter to the male (son) as the natural heir and hope for familial immortality. . . . It is during adolescence that the parents make it clear that intelligence and other talents of the daughter are now held by them as more quixotic than important."

The mother then becomes the chief "hatchet-woman" in this endeavor. She must, because she knows the secrets and tricks of "beauty," teach them to the daughter so that a husband may be won. Often, she must teach the daughter the work of the trade: how to cook, wash clothes, shop in the grocery store. There is no counterpart in the life of a boy. The mother or the father has no feeling that *he* must be made attractive physically in order to attract a wife; the boy's job is to do well in the world, and family resources are organized around helping him.

The most important job which the mother has is subtle. She must, by her own behavior and attitudes (Dr. Spock says it is crucial that children learn sex roles from their parents at an early age) teach the girl her place. Their place. No word need be spoken on this subject; if the

THE YOUNG WOMAN'S GUIDE TO LIBERATION

mother waits on the family, has no career of her own, lives through her husband and children, and appears to derive her identity and pleasures in life via other people, the message is carefully taught, and thoroughly learned. The daughter sees what she will be when she grows up, no matter how bright, artistic, scholarly, or beautiful she is. She will be a mother, and she will live to serve.

Dr. Bruno Bettelheim[5] stated clearly that a woman is judged as a failure if she does not marry fairly soon in life, no matter how successful or gifted she is in her work. "Motherhood was depicted to her . . . as another tremendous enlarging experience, while in reality it forces her to give up most of her old interests." Dr. Bettelheim suggested as one solution to freeing women "creating something akin to the extended family by entrusting part of infant care to older children or sharing it with relatives."

In relations with your mother, it is essential that you realize the trap that she is in. If it is at all possible, the female children of the family should take it as their special responsibility to help the mother break out of her cage: encourage her to go go back to school, encourage her to work, and try to get the household tasks shared by all members of the family—male and female. However, this is an ideal and will rarely be realized. In addition, it is not the duty of children to tell their parents what to do; it *is*, however, the duty of every female to help every other female. So, if a mother shows signs of wanting to assert herself, she needs all the help she can get. She will in all probability not be getting help from your father, so resist the standard father-daughter alliance and do not side against your mother. I have heard very bright, and basically kind, men say to working wives that they didn't mind "if she cooked their dinner late, they would understand."

The work that the housewife does not only looks dull;

it *is* dull. When someone does dull work, out of the mainstream of the world for years and years, she becomes dull. This is why fathers often are more interesting to their daughters than are mothers. However, no daughter should be misled into thinking that men are better and more interesting. Women, your mothers are a product of political oppression, and should be understood as such.

Many of us will have mothers who do not "want" to break out of the cage. My suggestion is to leave them alone. What they need is the love and understanding and compassion of other women, especially their own daughters. Moses stayed in the desert for forty years, although the walk from Egypt to Jerusalem did not take that long. He stayed in the desert because he didn't want his new nation to be formed by people who had lived as slaves. And so he walked around until all those who had been born in slavery had died of old age. Self-determination and decision-making cannot easily become the life style of a slave people.

In the final analysis, the best thing we can do for our mothers is not to try to change them, but to liberate ourselves. If we are uneasy around our own mothers it is because they are the closest living example of what the world does to women—and this makes us, if we are at all sensitive, very uptight. No blow is greater to a young woman who tells her mother of some accomplishment, than to be asked in return: "Who made dinner for your husband?"

If you have enough self-love, even that question will not destroy you. For, there but for the grace of Betty Friedan, go *you*.

NOTES TO CHAPTER VI

1. NOW Conference on Women's Employment, Chicago, Illinois, January 24, 1970.
2. deRham, Edith. *The Love Fraud*, New York: Clarkson N. Potter, Inc. Publisher, 1965, p. 213.
3. *New York Times*, June 27, 1970.
4. Dr. Robert Seidenberg. "The Case of the Missing Mind: Feminine Sexuality and the Adolescent Identity," *Nickel Review*, May 18, 1970.
5. Speech delivered in Durham, N.C., "The Change in Woman's Role in Home and Society." Reported in *Miami Herald*, June 1970.

CHAPTER VII

6,000 Years of Disenfranchisement: Women in Politics, or Rather, Women Not in Politics

W HENEVER anyone attempts a discussion on women in politics, it should be cut short, until certain facts of life are made clear: Women are not in politics. The proof is easily established. Point out who is the President of the United States, the governor of your state, the mayor of your city. Cite the number of women in the city council, in the state legislature, in the U.S. Congress. Point out who makes the laws, and who enforces them. The answer to all these questions is: men.

You will then be told that you elect these men. A short analysis is in order to show how the vote really did not advance the cause of women in this country, despite the difficult and brave work of the women who won the vote for us. Some of the early suffragists knew that our position in the United States would not change if we simply got the vote; the revolution must take place in the economic and political structure of the male supremacist society. And in the family.

We have had the vote for fifty years, and during that time we have consistently voted men into office to determine the course of our lives. There are many reasons for our doing this; among them is not that women are inferior politically.

Only four women have served as prime ministers of their countries during the twentieth century: Indira Gandhi of India, Golda Meir of Israel, Ana Pauker of Romania, and Mme. Bandaranaike of Ceylon. Victoria Woodhull of New York was the first woman to run for President of the United States in 1872 on the Peoples Party ticket. Since that time, several women have run for President, but never on parties which had a chance of winning. Politicians are eager to have women run for office if there is no chance of winning the district, or if the job is no good, or if no man wants it. Therefore, although few women actually run for office, fewer still win elections.

If this chapter has one point to drive home it is that the male supremacist world in which we live shows itself most explicitly in the political arena. Women are absent from decision-making positions, so absent that we hardly notice it ourselves. This is not a function of the capitalist system. This is not a function of a particular time in history. It has always been.

In many countries today, women are better off than we are in the United States. In Germany and Finland, 15% of Parliament are women. In the U.S., thirteen out of 435 members of the House of Representatives are women. Russia, in 1959, had 20 million more women than men in the Communist Party. Yet, only 17% of the delegates to the Party Congress were women. Since we got the vote, only ten women have served as U.S. Senators, and only five of these were elected[1] on their own. Women now hold less than 2% of the legislative posts in this country.

But in no country in the world are women equal to men in holding decision-making positions.

Discrimination against women takes place in political institutions, from the Republican Party to the Cuban National Committee. Mrs. Gladys O'Donnell, president of the National Federation of Republican Women, said[2] "I attended three days of hearings of the subcommittee on Constitutional Amendments. Under consideration was the Equal Rights Amendment. The testimony presented there by working and professional women from across the nation, supported by briefs from innumerable court cases, proved conclusively a degree of discrimination against women almost unbelievable in this century." After the last presidential nominating convention, *Life* magazine ran a picture-story "Democratic National Committee Meets and Makes Big Decisions." Page after page showed groups of men together in bedrooms, in bars—smoking and making big decisions. The last page showed the women. "Women Members of the National Committee Arrange Flowers for the Banquet." Women at the party conventions typically call the roll and sing the "Star-Spangled Banner." And arrange the flowers.

In Cuba, there are 100 persons on the National Committee. Two of these are women. "Machismo" is not only a Latin phenomenon. I spoke to one of these two women, who told me that although lip service is definitely paid to women's equality by the male members of the National Committee (which is more than men in the Congress of the United States would attest to), most of these men like their wives to be at home. A young woman I know in the United States told me that in her work in peace and civil rights movements, she found that the boys paid lip service to women's liberation, but that they liked "their chicks" to be docile and unliberated.

Not one country polled by the United Nations (March

1969) indicated that women have equality with men, although many countries have sex equality in the law. Legal equality does not exist in the United States today. We have thousands of laws which discriminate against women. In addition, our cases are fought in court by male lawyers (3% of the attorneys are female), and decided by male judges. Discriminatory laws hold that women are children, seen as needing protection. This means that many of our states have so-called "protective" laws, which prevent women from working overtime or from lifting more than 30 pounds, and which serve to keep us from holding down the higher-paying jobs, and often, the administrative positions. Discriminatory laws hold that women are evil. The best example of this are the abortion laws. It takes two to produce a baby, but the woman is penalized, by being forced (in most states) to bear unwanted children. Another good example of woman as the evil witch, are the prostitution laws. Mayors love to round up the prostitutes; it makes their administration seem to be against crime. However, the men who patronize the prostitutes are not usually penalized. Discriminatory laws hold that man and woman are one in marriage, and that one is the man. Women must take their husband's name, or go through endless redtape to keep their own. The property laws are hangovers from the middle ages, when women were chattel. A married woman cannot run for public office in a location other than where her husband lives. This means that if I teach at a university fifty miles from (my husband's) home, I cannot run for state assembly from that community. The most discriminatory laws hold that women are non-persons. There have been hundreds of decisions in the courts which show clearly that the equal protection clause of the Fourteenth Amendment does not apply to women. One example of this is the series of laws in most states that permit public accommodations to discriminate against women, prohibiting us from entering certain restaurants, bars, and hotels.

There is a logical reason why laws which discriminate against women exist: the laws are made by men, the laws are administered by men. At the Democratic and Republican party conventions in 1968, as in past years, there were almost no women delegates. When the women did speak, they were listed on the program as giving "remarks," while the men's presentations were listed as "speeches." Although women do most of the work of political organizations in America—envelope stuffing, telephoning, door-to-door canvassing, office work—we do not hold office.

Representative Shirley Chisholm (who has said publicly many times that she has been more discriminated against in her political life as a *woman* than as a black person) testified before a House subcommittee investigating sex discrimination: (reported 7/12/70) "Without his [the male politician's] thousands of women volunteers, the American party system would not work. It would break down in a confusion of unanswered letters, unmade phone calls, unkept appointments, unwritten speeches, and unheld meetings."

We are also not present at the decision-making sessions which informally determine political policy, and laws. In Syracuse, New York, for example, there are several committeewomen in one of the major political parties. All the major decisions of that party, however, are made after the regular committee meetings, when the men gather at a men-only bar.

The policies which are determined in these male smoked-filled rooms determine the quality of our lives. Laws on abortion, contraception, employment, education, and public accommodations are developed for us, without our presence. This nonrepresentation is not only a fact in the Establishment; it is also true in the Old Left, and in the New Left. Many members of the women's liberation movement realized the facts of male supremacy while working in the peace movement, the black civil rights movement, and in student revolts. They had been given the usual second-class roles and realized to their horror that they were encouraged to fight for other people's rights but not for their own.

Making coffee, not policy, starts very young in life. In the typical coeducational school, the president is a boy, the secretary is a girl.[3] At Syracuse University, the dean of women made a statement (February 1970) in favor of sororities: "Now that the women's student government at Syracuse University has dissolved itself, sororities provide the only arena for women to develop as leaders. Dormitories were granted autonomy last year, and without guaranteed offices, female independents find it hard to be elected to high offices on the interdormitory council."

We live in a male-run world, even in college. One thing that impressed me tremendously during the student strikes in spring 1970 was the male quality of the whole business. I watched countless television programs, local and national, in which views on the strike were being presented: students for the strike, students against the strike, college administrators, professors, politicians. And they were all males! A typical scene at Syracuse University, where I went to participate in the strike activity, was a student (invariably male) making a speech, surrounded by other students (males and females). While the students were so conscious of oppression—the oppression of American foreign policy in southeast Asia, the oppression of the American system toward the Black Panthers, the oppression of university administrators to students—striking students, both male and female, seemed to be innocent of the nonexistent position of women, the oppression of half their number. Whereas the students in America have recognized the mockery of their elders in regard to racism, they have not in regard to sexism.

Both major political parties have a rule that each state must have a woman vice-chairman and a national committeewoman. But she is simply head of the ladies auxiliary. "We're not supposed to deal with the issues," Mary Brooks, head of the Republican women's division, told Betty Friedan. "I'm so sick of fashion shows." In both parties, no matter how much political housework they do, women are not taken seriously.

Before the 1968 Presidential election, Mrs. Humphrey drank gallons of coffee with Democratic women, but both Humphrey and Muskie laughingly avoided answering a question directed to them on the Election Eve telethon as to their views on contraception and abortion. During his campaign, Mr. Nixon ignored all queries about contraception, abortion, the equal rights amendment, federally-sponsored child care centers, and policing the enforcement of Title VII (equality in employment) of the Civil Rights Act of 1964.

The Nixon administration is (still) under fire for weakness in enforcing the law guaranteeing women equal job opportunities in firms doing business with the federal government (*Miami Herald*, July 17, 1970). "Both Congress and women's rights groups are accusing the administration of lack of commitment to the goals embodied in two presidential orders."[4] Rep. Edith Green (Democrat, Oregon) accused the Justice Department of the "biggest copout of the century" in carrying out equal rights laws and executive orders."

When Angelina Grimke, a suffragist of the last century, accepted an offer that was meant as a joke and spoke before the Massachusetts legislature on the anti-slavery petitions, she was the first women ever to appear before a legislative body in the United States. A pastoral letter denounced her unwomanly behavior. ". . . If the vine, whose strength and beauty is to lean on the trellis-work and half conceal its cluster, thinks to assume the independence and overshadowing nature of the elm, it will not only cease to bear fruit, but fall in shame and dishonor in the dust."

A recent statement from the First Lady, Mrs. Patricia Nixon[5], would cause Angelina Grimke to fall in shame and dishonor: "Pat Nixon is all for women's equal rights —as long as her husband says so. . . . That seems to be the First Lady's position on the equal rights amendment pending in Congress."

If the woman suffrage movement in America has an identifiable beginning, it was in July 1848, at the first women's rights convention in Seneca Falls, New York. The Declaration of Sentiments is the most famous document in the history of feminism.

> When, in the course of human events, it becomes necessary for one portion of the family of man to assume among the people of the earth a position different from that which they have hitherto occupied, but one to which the laws of nature and of nature's God entitle them, a decent respect to the opinions of mankind requires that they should declare the causes that impel them to such a course . . .
>
> We hold these truths to be self-evident: that all men and women are created equal. . . . but when a long train of abuses and usurpations, pursuing invariably the same object, evinces a design to reduce them under absolute despotism, it is their duty to throw off such government, and to provide new guards for their future security. Such has been the patient sufferance of the women under this government, and such is now the necessity which constrains them to demand the equal station to which they are entitled. . . .
>
> The history of mankind is a history of repeated in-

juries and usurpations on the part of man toward woman, having in direct object the establishment of an absolute tyranny over her. To prove this, let facts be submitted to a candid world . . .

He has compelled her to submit to laws, in the formation of which she has had no voice . . .

He allows her in Church, as well as State, but in a subordinate position, claiming Apostolic authority for her exclusion from the ministry, and, with some exceptions, from any public participation in the affairs of the Church . . .

He has created a false public sentiment by giving to the world a different code of morals for men and women, by which moral delinquencies which exclude women from society, are not only tolerated, but deemed of little account in man.

He has endeavored, in every way that he could, to destroy her confidence in her own powers, to lessen her self-respect, and to make her willing to lead a dependent and abject life.

The following editorial appeared in the *New York Herald* (September 12, 1852), commenting upon the Declaration of Women's Rights drafted by Elizabeth Cady Stanton and Lucretia Mott.

The farce at Syracuse [near Seneca Falls] has been played out . . .

Who are these women? What do they want? What are the motives that impel them to this course of action? . . . some, having so much of the virago in their disposition, that nature appears to have made a mistake in their gender—mannish women, like hens that crow; some of boundless vanity and egotism, who believe that they are superior in intellectual ability to "all the world and the rest of mankind," and delight to see their speeches and addresses in print; and man shall be consigned to his proper sphere—nursing the babies, washing the dishes, mending stockings, and sweeping the house. This is "the good time coming."

How did woman first become subject to man as she now is all over the world? By her nature, her sex, just as the negro is and always will be, to the end of time, inferior to the white race, and, therefore, doomed to subjection; but happier than she would be in any other condition, just because it is the law of her nature.

Orestes A. Brownson wrote "The Woman Question," in the *Catholic World*, May, 1869:

. . . We do not believe women . . . are fit to have their own head. . . . Revelation asserts, and universal experience proves, that the man is the head of the woman, and that the woman is for the man, not the man for the woman; and that his greatest error, as well as the primal curse of society is that he abdicates his headship, and allows himself to be governed, we might almost say, deprived of his reason, by woman. It was through the seductions of the woman, herself seduced by the serpent, that man fell, and brought sin and all our woe into the world. She has all the qualities that fit her to be a help-meet of man, to be the mother of his children, to be their nurse, their early instructress, their guardian, their life-long friend; to be his companion, his comforter, his consoler in sorrow, his friend in trouble, his ministering angel in sickness, but as an independent existence, free to follow her own fancies and vague longings, her own ambition and natural love of power, without masculine direction or control, she is out of her element, and a social anomaly, sometimes a hideous monster, which men seldom are, excepting through a woman's influence.

It is hard to imagine how any man in his right mind would want a person who had brought all evil into the world to be the early instructress of his children, and his own comforter, but misogynists have their own brand of logic.

Have we come a long way, Baby? Have we ever.

Of some 1,200 appointments by President Nixon, only 15 have gone to women, and none is at the Cabinet level. The Report of the President's Task Force on Women's Rights and Responsibilities[6] states that "The President should appoint more women to positions of top responsibility in all branches of the federal government, to achieve a more equitable ratio of men and women. Cabinet and agency heads should be directed to issue firm instructions that qualified women receive equal consideration in hiring and promotions . . ."

But, 122 years after our sisters outlined where we "are not" in governing the country, we occupy basically the same position. We have had the vote for fifty years, but we have not voted for ourselves.

Press and political response to women's political equality seems interestingly consistent with that in the good old days. Jack Kofoed wrote in the *Miami Herald*[7]: "There can be no argument about equality. As for abortion, if a gal gets herself [sic] in a jam, all right, let the taxpayers pick up the tab. . . . If mom wants to work, or even jounce her fanny on a barstool, and drink up what pop is earning, why should I worry? . . . I love women. I want them to be happy, to have whatever education they really want, to get equal pay for equal jobs, even have abortions whenever they desire. . . . I've been happily married for 46 years . . . am a very happy man . . . love the fair and frail."

Philip Wylie is certain that we only want political power to ruin things for the men. "Although politics never interested her (unless she was exceptionally naive, a hairy foghorn, or a size forty scorpion) the damage she forthwith did to society was so enormous and so rapid that even the best men lost track of things."

It is not only men who feel there is something abhorrent about a woman having some say about her own destiny. Queen Victoria herself, apparently forgetting she was filling a "man's" role, said in 1860: "The Queen is most anxious to enlist everyone who can speak or write to join in checking this mad, wicked folly of Women's Rights, with all its attendant horrors, on which her poor, feeble sex is bent, forgetting every sense of womanly feeling and propriety."

Perhaps one of the fears which men have about women

in positions of political power is that when they imagine a female uprising they imagine a world in which women rule men as men have ruled women. And this would really be a disaster! Their guilt, which is the guilt of every ruling class, closes their eyes to the possibility of a society run on equitable principles, and actions.

How do women fare in the Revolution? Lenin's wife, Krupskaya, pushed a women's rights plank into his revolutionary theory (1917). The women's revolution, however, is not an accidental by-product of any economic revolution. Any society will elevate its women and will treat them equally while we are needed, but as soon as that need passes, women will go back to the same position we have always had, unless there has been some special preparation.

Russian women today, who are in definitely better positions than are American women in the professions and in industry, hold two jobs. They return at night to do the cooking and the cleaning. Their men still consider children the special province of the mother. Perhaps one of the saving graces for the Russian woman is shortage of housing; she has no ten-room trap to clean in the evening after work.

The SDS girls at Cornell (1968) wanted to pull out of the SDS and form their own women's liberation group because if they opened their mouths too aggressively within the SDS they didn't have dates! It was the feminine mystique all over again.

Francoise Parturier writes, in *Une Lettre Ouverte aux Hommes* (An Open Letter To Men), about how revolution doesn't mean freedom for women: "In 1789, we had the French Revolution—for men. Before that, the women, some of them at least, were very well educated. This of course was in the high society, the bourgeoise society. They knew Latin, Greek, philosophy. Some of them fought together with the men against the prejudice and the privileges of the Old Regime. And when the men had victory, what did they do? They made a law—it is incredible, but it is true—which said that all girls must cease going to school at the age of 8."

The *Women's Liberation Resolution,* passed at SDS, National Council, December, 1968:

> Women form the oldest and largest continually oppressed group in the family of humankind, their subjugation dating from the downfall of primitive communal society and the rise of private property . . .
>
> Male supremacy in the movement mirrors male supremacy in capitalist society.
>
> In order for women to become full political people in SDS, and in order for the oppression of women to be taken on as a struggle by SDS, male supremacy must be eliminated within the organization itself. SDS people must battle two beliefs. First, women in SDS must battle the belief that struggling for their own liberation is not important. Second, SDS must battle the belief that the fight for equality of women is solely the business of women, and that only women have the right and responsibility to oppose male domination.

Women who fought against slavery over 100 years ago were told not to press their own claims, at that time, for the vote. When the racial question was solved, we would get our turn. We did not get the vote until 1920. Women were urged, during the period around World War I, not to press their own selfish claims, but to work instead for world peace. Women were told in the 1960s that the priority in this country is black rights, and that women's rights is not where good liberal/radical energies should be spent. Women today are being told that the war, or the Black Panthers, or air pollution—you name it—is the problem.

Fortunately we are getting ourselves together. No one

will tell us where the priorities are. We know. Our priorities are in getting our own human status.

The last election year where millions of women went to the polls to vote for the Best Man was 1970. From now on we are voting for ourselves.

NOTES TO CHAPTER VII

1. The other five were widows of elected Senators who died in office. Margaret Chase Smith is the single example of a woman who was appointed to fill out her husband's term, and then went on to win several elections on her own.
2. Reported in the *Miami Herald*, July 3, 1970.
3. This will change in the near future. The Future Politicians of America is attempting to prepare young women for politics, much in the same way that Future Teachers of America prepares them for teaching. Among its goals are: a) to train young women to run for school office, in preparation for college politics and national politics; b) to train young women to be Congressional and Senate pages; c) to work on the campaigns of women running for public office; and d) to monitor sexism in the schools, as it appears in textbooks, in allocation of school budgets, etc.
4. *Miami Herald*, July 17, 1970.
5. *Syracuse Herald-Journal*, April 29, 1970.
6. Report of the President's Task Force on Women's Rights and Responsibilities, April 1970, p. 28.
7. *Miami Herald*, July 17, 1970.

CHAPTER VIII

What the "Helping" Professions Tell You about Being a Woman

I N 1869 JOHN STUART MILL wrote "The Subjection of Women." In it, he compared the status of the wife in Western marriage to that of the black slave in America, and said that man's "happiness" in love was dependent upon having a willing slave to serve his needs. It was, he said, to the advantage of the husband, like the slave-owner, to take good care of the wife (slave); neither wife nor slave had the power to make decisions about his/her own life, and each had a total lack of economic (money) and political power. Freud's wife-to-be, Martha, wrote to him that she found Mill's essay intriguing. He answered her that she should not trouble her little head with such heavy thoughts, and that after the joyous day of their marriage she could concern herself with keeping their home a place of peace and loveliness.

Since then, it has been very difficult for women on the analyst's couch. Freud himself, at the end of his life, wrote that although more than half of his patients were female, he found that he understood their sexuality, but did not understand them as human beings. The understanding of women was, he said, something perhaps best left to the poets and philosophers.

A practicing psychoanalyst[1] writes: ". . . Freud was quite explicit in the limitations of the psychoanalytic contribution. . . . [He] saw the woman in biological terms and did not see her in social and worldly dimensions. In this he reflected the mood and spirit of his time and those which preceded him. Thus Freud saw the adolescent girl's principle problem as identifying herself to her future role in marriage, child raising and domesticity. If she did well in these, she was considered healthy—if she rebelled or couldn't 'identify' she was both troubled and in trouble."

Freud did not invent the concept of the uterus-as-key-to-health. Just as it is assumed today (by therapists, by the person in the street) that a good way to cure depression in a woman is for her to get pregnant, from Hippocrates' time onward, the cure for hysteria was pregnancy. "There has been a basic assumption that the biological role was the one that transcended all oth ־s and which would totally suffice for [the woman's] living and gratification. We have always been willing to diagnose women as abnormal or have them under a pale of suspicion if some did not conform to what the male dominant society thought was good for them."[2]

When women aspire to any role other than biological, they are met with reactions of fear, derision, or sometimes, merely puzzlement.

It is interesting to note that just as Freud wondered what it is "you women want," the (usually) men in the so-called helping professions have continued to wonder the same thing. This question, very similar in effect to asking "what do you niggers want" of the black person, is also asked with intent looks by husbands and lovers, and is also asked with politically-pleasing smiles by legis-lators and government executives. The answers which these questioners supply themselves are typically 180° away from what it is that we women really do want; however, the most offensive part of the dialogue is that the question is asked at all. It is inherently condescending in nature (come now, little girl, tell big daddy your troubles) and also implies a total lack of understanding of another segment of humanity: female.

However, when it comes to the therapists, the question is more than offensive—it is downright dangerous.

A friend working happily on her doctoral disserta-tion at a large prestigious midwestern university was at age twenty-five not married. She had men friends, she was involved in her work; her family was, "naturally," ter-ribly disturbed that she would be an old maid, and since she is a sensitive person, this disquiet got to her. She presented to an analyst the problem that she was pur-suing her career, was unmarried, and did not want to get married, at least then, but wanted to finish her PhD. After she and the analyst worked on the problem for a few years, she stopped work on the dissertation (she never finished it) and she got married.

Another friend, age forty and working at a major publishing house in New York at $17,000 a year (a salary that exceeds what all but .1% of the working women in America earn), is in her second analysis. She is a productive and happy person, but her problem is that she doesn't want to get pregnant, and it is hoped that where her first analyst failed (to convince her that preg-nancy, childbirth, and motherhood are the answers to mental health and happiness), her second may succeed.

Still another woman, desirous of becoming an actress, told her analyst that she wanted to work through the problem of being terrified at auditions. She felt she should become more self-confident and be able to meet new people and enter new situations with less anxiety. He told her that her desire to become an actress was narcissistic, and advised her to stay where she belonged, to take care of her husband and children. She, fortunately, got up off the couch that day, and never returned.

I fully realize that the above cases are anecdotal evidence. We all know there are analysts who do not consider marriage and child-raising to be the exclusive goal of every woman. We also know that there are many types of professionals in the field: psychoanalysts, psychiatrists, psychiatric social workers, clinical psychologists, etc. Each has a particular set of professional dogma.

But the women in women's liberation, because of their own experience with men in the helping professions, have concluded almost unanimously, that the extent of liberation which most women can obtain from most of these men is the freedom to enjoy sex and the freedom to enjoy the inner world. As to the freedom to enjoy the outer world, which is, in the final analysis, where the *real* fun is, more women have been turned off than have been turned on. For this reason, it is dangerous, on the whole, for young women to go into psychoanalysis. Unmarried women are suspect from the start. The idea that some female doesn't want to change her name, move to the city of someone else's choice, and cook dinner seven nights a week is interpreted, instead of as a sign of health and independence, as a sign of trouble. Why are you resisting being a woman?

Resistance to having children is interpreted, not as a healthy assertion of self and a recognition that in a society with no child care facilities the mother effectively gives up her own identity for ten to fifteen years to care for other people, but as a symptom of sickness. Why are you resisting being a woman? Do you not know that the function of a woman is to bear children?

Although psychoanalysis is a "luxury" of very few Americans, it has effects far beyond the small number of people who can afford the couch. First of all, the people who can afford to go to the psychoanalyst are the potential leaders of the society, *by virtue of their money*. We pay, in this day and age, some lip service to open enrollment policies at the city university, but everyone really knows that it is the people with money who can afford the education and have the connections to win political power and most often, who have in adulthood the prestigious jobs which their fathers had when they were children. Therefore, whereas the *men* who go to the psychoanalyst typically emerge healthy enough to pursue their careers without the blocks of uncertainty about their own abilities, and hence to become the leaders of the society, the *women* who go through psychoanalysis emerge to become the *wives* of these men.

Secondly, and perhaps more important, is the fact that the psychoanalytic doctrines have passed (watered down and distorted, perhaps) into educational psychology, into the social sciences, and into the guides on child-raising. A key dogma in psychoanalytic theory is that of the importance, almost sanctity, of sex differences. Freud said "anatomy is destiny"; his disciples not only concur in this belief, but lend the patina of a very prestigious profession to the spread of this doctrine in the educational system.

Dr. Spock, for example, who has thought, spoken, and behaved so bravely on the subjects of youth, civil liberties, the right to dissent, and so on, is oppressive on the subject of women. He, and other child care experts, also write on and on about how Mommy must act like a woman and Daddy must act like a man, or else baby will be confused and disturbed. This is all fine, except what it means in practice is that baby boy learns that he will go out and be a lawyer or an electrician, and baby girl learns that she (despite great report cards and high IQ scores) will be, in twenty years, watching the new soap powder clean the shirt collars white. Such learning is dangerous for young women, and for this reason, women must develop an awareness of the effect that the myth of sex role identification has on their lives.

Recently I attended a meeting entitled "Women's Liberation and Psychoanalysis." The program consisted of two papers delivered by women, one a psychoanalyst, the other a psychologist, to an audience of practicing psychoanalysts (all male) and members of NOW and other women in the movement. The psychoanalyst discussed "femininity"; the psychologist gave a review of the literature on sex role differences and suggested that we re-examine the conclusions drawn about mental health for women. Following the papers, various women in the group made comments which, although spoken with courtesy, indicated that we felt that the profession of psychoanalysis served as a political, if you will, oppressor to women, by defining our sphere as "children, church, and kitchen." To illustrate our points, we used anecdotal evidence—experiences we had had or heard of from the thousands of women we talk to about freedom for women.

The psychoanalysts were furious: at being attacked, and at being bombarded with anecdotal evidence. We were all amused, particularly, at the latter, since of course the psychoanalytic literature consists of anecdotal evidence exclusively. Obviously, these men liked their anecdotes, not ours.

When I left the meeting I was convinced that the problem between women's liberation and psychoanalysis was not one of lack of communication; it was that we have different ideologies. A significant example of this is that one of the doctors defined his job as helping people to "do their work . . . helping them to perform what they do."

The major problem which women have is not psychological, it is political. Our work, what we do, is awful. We scrub the floors, we cook the meals, we carry the groceries, we wipe the noses, we type the papers, we clean up the operating room, we file the legal documents. Therefore, any doctor trying to help us perform our work better will succeed in making gourmet cooks from women who used to burn the hamburgers, and speeding up our typing rate. This is utter nonsense. Our revolution consists redefining our work, changing it, beginning to do the creative work of the world.

Another unfortunate assumption of those in the "helping professions" is that of female passivity and male dominance. By some strange leap of logic, sexual positions in bed (which in actuality have little relationship to female passivity and male dominance) are translated into the world at large. Standards for mental health of healthy adults are similar to standards for mental health of healthy *males* (aggressiveness, shaping the earth to suit you); for females mental health is defined differently. A study was recently done[3] in which psychologists gave a sex-role stereotype questionnaire to 79 clinicians with one of three sets of instructions: to describe a healthy, mature, socially competent (a) adult, sex unspecified, (b) a man, or (c) a woman. It was hypothesized that clinical judgments about the characteristics of healthy individuals would differ as a function of sex of person judged, and that these differences would parallel stereotypic sex-role differences. A second hypothesis predicted that behaviors and characteristics judged healthy for an adult, sex unspecified, which are presumed to reflect an ideal standard of health, will resemble behaviors judged healthy for men, but not for women. Both hypotheses were confirmed.

Each of us can think quickly of women of extraordinary competence who stay in the home all day, tending the children and the garden. If one simply substitutes mentally the image of a man with the same capabilities and often, with the same level of education, and places him doing the same task, we can see immediately that he would be an instant candidate for the psychoanalyst's couch, or perhaps even a mental hospital.

Here we have thirty-year-old Mr. A. He is a college graduate, he has an IQ of 130. He stays in the home all day. He cooks, he cleans, he gardens. He reads the newspaper when the children are quiet for ten minutes; he reads his magazines in the evening—on how to cook more attractive meals and how to make his flowers grow better. His magazines also contain articles on how to keep his wife charmed in three dozen new and exciting ways. He plans, when the children are grown up in twenty years, to go out and get a job. Right now, he goes out once a week to do the family grocery shopping, and once a month to buy underwear for the family at the department store. He also plays cards with his friends once a week.

A ghastly picture, one which we would all realize immediately as requiring instant psychiatric care. Mr. A. has retreated from the world, into passivity. We will all call him sick. Mrs. A., however, can live this life and everyone thinks that she is fine.

Erik Erikson talks of inner space being the special domain of women, and of outer space (the city, the moon) being the domain of men. If one is being gentle and gracious, one can say that this kind of analysis is limiting to women. If one is being perhaps more direct, one can say that this kind of analysis is developed with brilliance and precision by those persons who enjoy running outer space (the city, the country, the corporations, and the medical profession), to keep others down.

What women have decided is that we can no longer allow men to define what is mental health for us. We will decide this ourselves. At the moment, since women have been *treated* differently for 6,000 years, it is impossible to tell what the real sex differences are—if they exist and what their existence should imply for training people. At the moment, the definitions are written by men and enforced by men. The few women who are in the "helping professions" typically have had to undergo such bludgeoning themselves, in order to achieve in male-dominated professions, that they accept the dogma without question, or else they consider themselves the exceptions to the dogma they are teaching (I am creative and imaginative and would atrophy in the kitchen, but most other women are well suited for it); a few work diligently within the professional structure to change dogma and practice. Even the last has its difficulties, because as long as we are playing within the game which was set up to preserve male dominance, and playing within the rules enough to be allowed to stay in the game, we are often being co-opted from seeing our own true self-interest.

We cannot be abused any longer by the myths of so-called scientific inquiry. The literature shows that men are better suited to run the country. Prove that they are not. Use the research methods that men have set up; write up your experiment in the acceptable manner; and (best yet) you must convince the men that your conclusions are correct. All this is not only nonsense, it will never work.

Women will define what is mental health for women. Women will say to the male psychoanalysts and psychiatrists that we don't even care what their definitions are. If they say it is healthy to like the cotton field, we will say forget it.

The psychological professions have never fully examined whether the traits thought to be feminine are truly innate, and biological, or merely culturally learned and reinforced. Psychology merely accepts and reinforces society's prejudices and then uses case histories and eyeball-blink measurements to back them up. The idea that women are naturally emotional, motherly, loving, passive, and that biology (the equipment to conceive a child) controls our mental processes is a big brainwash.

It is time for us to tell the psychoanalysts that the Big Trauma comes not in the bathroom, where the little girl is supposedly damaged psychologically, upon discovering that her brother has a penis and she does not, but in the living room, while the family watches the evening news, and the little girl discovers who is giving the news, and more important, who is *making* the news.

It is not she.

NOTES TO CHAPTER VIII

1. Seidenberg, *op. cit.*
2. Seidenberg, Ibid.
3. Broverman, Inge K. et al, Worcester State Hospital, Massachusetts, *Sex-role stereotypes and clinical judgments of mental health.* Journal of Consulting & Clinical Psychology, 1970, 34 (1), 1–7.

CHAPTER IX

The School for Wives: Dating

THE LESSON of what a woman is, is learned very well in the family. The lesson is reinforced in school, in Sunday school, by the television programs. But its true message cannot possibly sink in to the consciousness of a young girl until she has some practice using her lessons. This practice begins on the first date.

Dating is a nightmare for both sexes, from beginning to end. But for females it is worse. A girl who doesn't date by age sixteen is considered strange, or a lesbian. Her mother is in a panic. Her friends are desperately trying to fix her up. If she is not a beauty queen, she is counseled to have her nose shortened, her skin sandpapered, her ears pinned back, her hair curled or straightened (depending on the fashion), and she is often sent to charm school.

"Be yourself, but be an improved you. Invest in contact lenses. Have your nose fixed, your ears pinned back, or your teeth capped. Whatever physical feature you can't live with, change or diminish. Get professional advice about cosmetics and clothes. If you're not very pretty, be well-read. If you're not intellectual or pretty, be athletic, charming, or charitable. Build yourself some assets. Concentrate on what's behind your smile and you'll find the smart man for you."[1]

No one is really talking about the "physical features" *you* can't stand. They are talking about the physical features which may stand between you and the boy of your dreams. Today's date; tomorrow's husband.

Infinitely more devastating to the young woman than primping herself up for the big date, however, is primping down her mind. Everyone knows that if you are really smart, you will act dumb. Girls are counseled by their parents, and by their friends, from preadolescence on, to lose at games. Don't be aggressive on the tennis court; don't win at scrabble. The more sensitive givers of such advice realize how grotesque it is, so they try to give a rationale: young boys are very insecure; they are particularly insecure about their relations with young girls; help them along during this trying period by catering to their insecurity; build them up by acting weak and helpless.

This is a particularly difficult chapter for me to write because of the intense suffering which my friends and I (all bright and achieving students) went through trying to act helpless and stupid enough to attract men. Beautiful girls suffer in this process because they are billed as sex objects and become so popular that they often cease to think of themselves as anything else. Unattractive girls suffer particularly, because they have to go through the tortures of the damned trying to make themselves beautiful. Or, worse yet, they have to develop these so-called "understanding" personalities (they become doormats for any male who honors them with his presence). Smart girls are told in no uncertain terms that boys don't like (date, marry) girls who become doctors and lawyers; they don't even like girls who talk a lot in class.

One fact which becomes crystal clear a few years after college is that the same males who needed all this bolstering while they were browbeaten medical students or underpaid junior employees, learn very quickly that male supremacy rules the world, and acquire the self-confidence that their wives and girl friends have been trying to instill in them all these years. So, the shy male of twenty (with the girl friend who tells him four times a day how wonderful he is) becomes the not-so-shy male of thirty (with the wife who stays at home with three children while he is self-confidently moving up in his career). A social fact which no one seems to notice is that young women are also insecure. Human beings who have not been out in the world, and have not been able to achieve yet in any area (few are child movie stars), are of course insecure about their own capabilities. One never hears, however, how the young man should work hard to build up the ego of the young woman. Asking her out on a date is enough.

A boy who doesn't date at age sixteen is not considered strange; he is considered shy. As Sally Kempton points out[2]:

> . . . for adolescent boys, sexual success is not the sole measure of worth. It is assumed that they will grow up and work, that their most important tests will come in areas whose criteria are extra-sexual. They can fail with girls without failing entirely, for there remains for them the public life, the male life.
>
> But girls have no such comfort. Sex occupies even the economic center of our lives; it is, we have been brought up to feel, our lives' work. Whatever else she may do, a woman is a failure if she fails to please men. The adolescent girl's situation is by definition dependent; she *must* attract, and therefore, however she may disguise it, she must compromise the sticky edges of her personality, she

must arrange herself to conform with other people's ideas of what is valuable in a woman.

This pleasing of men has sexual, in addition to social and intellectual, connotations. At one time we women were chaste, because men wanted wives to be chaste. The Victorian concept of two kinds of women—whores and wives —was well integrated into American mores. So, women didn't go to bed before marriage because *men wanted it that way*. More recently we have had the so-called sexual revolution. It is only so-called, because it has not changed the relations between the sexes at all. Men now want women who are great in bed. So, girls study up on how to be great in bed. Virginity is no longer what the men want (most of them); athletic and participating bed partners is what they want. So, women go to bed before marriage because *men want it that way*.

Sexual freedom for women would mean, of course, that a woman could choose to be celibate, to sleep with one man, to sleep with many men—because *she wanted it that way*. It is very important to recognize that the sexual revolution has not changed our lives. A man I know, perceptive in many areas of life, told me that he thought the feminists would like the Playboy philosophy because it advocated sexual freedom. He had apparently fallen into the trap which so many of us also fall into: equating going to bed with sexual freedom.

We will be free sexually when we can choose when to go to bed, and with whom. Sex today is similar to other activities in male-female relations. We all are taught that when a man wants to talk, talk to him. No matter that you are studying, that you feel like being alone. It is the duty of a woman to talk to her man when he wants to communicate. On the other hand, men have important work and thinking to do. When a man wants silence, be silent. And, if there are children and dogs around, keep them quiet too. We all are taught that when a man wants to "do something," (go to the movies, play golf, visit friends) do it with him, if he wants your company, and let him do it alone if he wants to do it alone. Be sure, also, to pack sandwiches if desired, and have the house in order if he wants to have his friends over for a round of poker. When a man doesn't want to do something, leave him be. Only the nagging bitch tries to drag her poor husband or boyfriend to a party when he doesn't want to go.

Sex has now come into this general category of doing things. So, if the male wants sex, have it, or you will be considered frigid and sent to a psychiatrist. If the male doesn't want sex, don't want it either, or you will be considered over-sexed and sent to a psychiatrist.

These lessons are so taken for granted that we hardly know that we are learning them. A woman I know, married to a wealthy businessman, is trying to graduate from college by taking one course per semester (she will have her degree in time to enter the old people's home). When questioned why she doesn't go to college full-time and graduate soon, she replied that it is even difficult for her to take one course at a time. When her husband (who has a lot of free time because he is in such a high position in his firm) wants to play golf with her, or go out to dinner, or go to the movies, he becomes furious if she has to study.

This sense of privilege is carefully taught to males in our culture. John Stuart Mill[3] explains:

> The self-worship of the monarch, or of the feudal superior, is matched by the self-worship of the male. Human beings do not grow up from childhood in the possession of unearned distinctions, without pluming themselves upon them. Those whom privileges not acquired by their merit, and which they feel to be disproportioned to it, are al-

ways the few, and the very best. . . . Above all, when the feeling of being raised above the whole of the other sex is combined with personal authority over one individual among them; . . . and often revenge themselves upon the unfortunate wife for the involuntary restraint which they are obliged to submit to elsewhere.

A hundred years after Mill, perceptive men still feel the same way about unearned privilege.

Poet David Slavitt,[4] who uses the name Henry Sutton when writing novels, such as *The Exhibitionist,* says: "Men are organized . . . And we've got everything we want, much more than we have a right to. I've had everything I wanted for years." He compares men's viewing women to the aristocrat viewing the peasant in revolt. "We can see it's terribly unfair and has to change, but we would rather later than sooner. Privilege, aside from being morally indefensible, is terribly pleasant."

Men, even at a very young age, are aware of this privilege, and they aim to protect it. Male solidarity is recognized by women and men alike.

In *World of Profit,*[5] by Louis Auchincloss, some men are discussing an impending divorce, where both the lawyers for the husband and the wife are male (only 3% of the lawyers in the United States are female). "You're my lawyer. I need your judgment and your bargaining power. I need you to hammer some sense into Hulda's crazy head. She wants my shirt. Jay almost smiled as he saw John's frown. He knew he could count on the inarticulate loyalty that exists between all males in any prospective battle of the sexes."

Although male solidarity is recognized by everyone, female solidarity is a new thing. Women, traditionally, have had to work too hard *getting a man* to feel a sisterhood with the potential competition.

A new, nationally syndicated column (by Ellen Peck)

is called "How to get a teenage boy and what to do with him when you get him." *Seventeen Magazine,* May 1970, featured an article "Get Him to Notice Me?" The reader was counseled: "Is your voice a piping treble? Deep breathing will relax throat muscles. Next time an attractive man is near, look at him frankly, physically. Think sexy thoughts. . . . Try a more sophisticated hairdo." An article in the February 1970 issue of the same magazine contains assumptions which are worse than its message. "How to Get along with Boys," by Daniel A. Sugarman, PhD. and Rollie Hochstein tells its readers that

> . . . Boys are expected to be aggressive and competitive.
> A boy is responsible for proving himself, making his own way in life, while a girl is expected to marry into her role.
> A thoughtful girl doesn't deluge her boyfriend with girl talk (like maxis and midis). Take the trouble to learn the boy's language.
> A girl may be ready to play down her friendships in favor of a boyfriend, but most boys are not willing to cut down their time with all male groups.
> Enjoy being a girl. In our society, men are expected to provide for and take care of their women. And the girl who takes these prerogatives away from a man undermines his self-esteem. If you want to get along with boys, then you'll permit them to act out their manliness, whether it's opening doors for you or not opening doors for you.

Whereas the old-fashioned girl could just memorize that men always opened the door, the modern girl now must be sharper. If the boy wants to open doors, figure that out and let him. If the boy doesn't want to open doors, figure that out and do it yourself.

If you follow all these instructions, you can get (and keep) a date.

Ms. Coy[6] gives advice on how to avoid the ultimate failure: no date on a Saturday night.

Wednesdays are busy nights at singles bars because that's the 'scouting night,' when men line up weekend dates. Fridays are also good, since, after a long week's work, many men prefer to 'bounce' (bar-hop) rather than go through all the effort of having a date. Saturday afternoons jump as singles come in from the beach, tennis courts, or shopping. Saturday nights, however, tend to be flat, since no self-respecting girl will admit she's dateless on The Big Night.

Although the successful date/wife always familiarizes herself with the work situation of the male and can discuss it intelligently (or not discuss it, if he so prefers), she can have no illusions that her work is similarly in focus. As Rebecca E. Greer[7] explains: "Your job is an important part of your life, but it's still only one part. Try to succeed, but don't let it go to your head. Leave your office personality and your office problems in the office; they don't belong on dates. Men like intelligent, successful, and high-salaried women, but they don't like constant reminders of exactly how intelligent, successful, and high-salaried they are. The average man gets enough competition in his work; he doesn't need it on social occasions, too. Learn to keep your job in its place, and no man will have cause to put you in yours."

Men apparently like successful and high-salaried women on dates, but do not like them as wives. A study[8] found that "both males and females had become more accepting of a wife working, but males, almost without exception, projecting five and ten years into the future, desired a wife who was a homemaker only. About one half of the females shared this view."

The expectation that a daughter will not be the person to carry on or create the family fame is a condition in all social classes. An article[9] about Joe Kelly, a construction worker, discusses his political and social views, and his family. "There is his pretty blond wife, Karen; two strawberry blonde daughters, Robin Lynn, 4, and Kerry Ann, 1½, and now a newborn son, James Patrick. 'I had two cheerleaders,' he says, 'now I got a ballplayer.' " Mr. Kelly talks about the family future: "He would like his daughters to go to college or nursing school and his son to get as much schooling as possible to become a doctor or a lawyer—'something where he can use his head to make a living, not his back like his old man does.' "

The upper class also stratifies the life styles of males and females. In an article[10] on debutantes, one girl says: "Daddy is terrifically happy doing what he's doing, and Mummy is, well, not so happy, but like she says, 'Who else would do all the work there is in a family with five children?' "

Even those who are trying to do away with the myths surrounding sex, still keep the myth of the double standard. Masters and Johnson, at their sex clinic which helps men and women to overcome various sexual hangups, use a different standard for men and for women. They treat couples; and they treat single men—for whom they supply female sex partners. Single women are not treated, unless they bring their own sex partners. The rationale behind this is so ironic it is hilarious: Masters and Johnson claim that women are taught, that for them, sex belongs only in marriage, and that therefore treatment outside the marriage contract would complicate their problems. That they hope to "treat" sex problems without attacking perhaps the most important sex problem—the double standard—is amazingly naive.

No discussion of boys and dating would be complete without the addition that women can, of course, have a lot of fun with men. Working with men can be a lot of fun, just as working with women is. Talking to men can be a lot of fun, just as talking to women is. And of course sexual pleasure is a lot of fun. But this pleasure can best be insured, if a women remembers certain things. There is an old saying (of men) that women are all the same in the dark.

A new saying (of women) is that men are all the same in the light. What this means is that every male is trained from birth to think that females are put on earth to serve his needs, his pleasures. So, whether the rhetoric is from the athlete or the intellectual, it can be translated into the same words: the male is the organizing principle of the female's life. Once a young girl knows this fact of life, she need not get herself to a nunnery; she can live with, or without, men, without being destroyed. *She* can be the organizing principle of her own life.

NOTES TO CHAPTER IX

1. Coy, Stanlee Miller. *The Single Girl's Book: Making It in the Big City*, Englewood Cliffs, New Jersey: Prentice-Hall, Inc., 1969, p. 32.
2. Kempton, Sally, "Cutting Loose," *Esquire*, July, 1970, p. 54.
3. Mill, John Stuart, *op. cit.*
4. *Miami Herald*, May 31, 1970.
5. Auchincloss, Louis. *World of Profit*, Boston: Houghton Mifflin Co., 1968, p. 181.
6. Coy, Stanlee Miller, *op. cit.*, p. 34.
7. Greer, Rebecca E. *Why Isn't a Nice Girl Like You Married?*, New York: The Macmillan Company, 1969, p. 28.
8. Helen Y. Nelson and Phyllis R. Goldman, New York State College of Home Economics, Cornell University, "Attitudes of high school students and young adults toward the gainful employment of married women. *Family Coordinator*, 1969, 18 (3), 251–55.
9. *New York Times Magazine*, June 28, 1970, p. 12:
10. *New York Times*, July 5, 1970, p. 41.

CHAPTER X

Love and Marriage:
The Canary's Cage

THIS ECONOMIC dependence is the underlying ground of
the helplessness of women. . . . [N]o human creatures
can be free whose bread is in other hands than theirs. . . .
Husband, father, or brother may give wealth to wife,
daughter or sister—but that does not make her economically independent in the true sense. As well pile your
canary's cage with seed and sugar and say he is independent of your care. . . .

    Charlotte Perkins Gilman, *Economic Basis of the Woman
Question*, 1898

WRITING OVER seventy years ago, Charlotte Gilman
was one of the boldest thinkers among our suffragist
sisters. She realized early that the vote would not change
the life of women in America unless we could change our
economic condition. She also clearly recognized marriage
as the job to which women aspire because other jobs are
cut off to them. Excited by her times, during which in-
dustrialization was changing the face of the society, she
was appalled by the stagnant, primitive life of the home.[1]

A peculiar condition of women is that their environment has been almost wholly that of the home; and the home is the most ancient of human institutions; the most unalterably settled in its ideals and convictions; the slowest and last to move. . . . In our social world today, men and women who are familiar with liquefied air and Roentgen rays, who have accepted electric transit and look forward with complacence to air-ships, people who are as liberal and progressive in mechanical lines, remain sodden and buried in their prehistoric sentiment as to the domestic relations. The world of science and invention may change; art, religion, government may change; but women and the home are supposed to remain as they are, forever. . . .

Mrs. Gilman, who died in 1935, would now have to revise her essays to include the facts that hearts are transplanted and men walk on the moon. But her definition of women as domestic servants would still be correct. Women waited on men thousands of years ago, we waited on men under Mrs. Gilman's eye, and we still do. And ". . . domestic service is the lowest grade of labor remaining extant. It belongs to an earlier social era. . . . When a man marries a housemaid, makes a wife of his servant, he alters her social status; but if she continues in the same industry he does not alter her economic status."[2]

In a 1912 article,[3] Mrs. Gilman explains why women have accepted for so long the male definitions of women's humanity:

Whether in the accumulated literature of the necessarily unenlightened past, or the still accumulated literature of the wilfully unenlighted present, we find everywhere this same pervasive error, this naive assumption, which would be so insolent if it were not so absurd, that only men are human creatures, able and entitled to perform the work of the world; while women are only female creatures, able to do nothing whatever but continue in the same round of duties to which they have been so long restricted.

They darkly threaten, do these ultra male opponents,

that if women persist in doing human things they will lose the respect of man—yea, more, they will lose his pecuniary support.

Indeed, probably the reason why marriage as an institution has survived through the years is that women cannot earn a living. But the young girl growing up is not told that. She learns in subtle ways that she is not expected to make a career for herself, to earn her way in the world. What she is told blatantly is that her whole success is dependent on winning a man. Any female of age twelve who doesn't know this, has been living on a desert island.

Better to be dead than not to be wed. Louis Auchincloss, in *World of Profit*[4] describes the plight of the single woman.

A female character says, "You can't put yourself in the shoes of a girl who's over thirty and unmarried. . . . I certainly make no claim that Mr. Livingston is a catch, but I suggest *you* find us a better. You've always gone on about Sophie being your darling. Let's see what you'll do for her now!"

A not-so-good husband is better than none at all. In earlier periods, when individual freedom was not as highly valued, marriages were arranged, and openly stated to be part of the family design. Romantic love is a recent invention, and serves to cloud the economic base for marriage.

To be oppressed through hate is at least understood. To be oppressed through economic necessity is also comprehensible. But to be oppressed through love is the most dangerous of all. When a man says "I love you," inherent in the statement is that he thinks (and you think) you will do the shopping, cooking, and cleaning until death do you part. This kind of work might be done by persons who cannot earn their livelihood in any other way.

But today there are many women who can earn (if not as much as their male counterparts) a living. The only way these women could possibly be induced to do domestic work, and to submerge their personalities, is via the myth of love.

Shakespeare said that men have died and worms have eaten them, but not for love. This may not be true for women. We are taught from early childhood that we are meant for love. We learn this from our mothers, from the books we read, from the movies we see, and from the songs we sing.

A popular song, high on the charts in summer 1970 (Bobbie Barton, vocalist): "If you love him, make him your reason for living." The disc jockey at a Syracuse station added at the end of the song, "You'd better, or he'll cut off the grocery money." Apparently, the economic bases for love are not as secret as one might think.

Being in love is the state to which all women must aspire. When a young girl is asked "What is new?" no one is asking if her essay won a prize. They mean does she have a boyfriend, is she in love. Any woman who is not in love is to pitied. Nothing is too important to supersede a love relationship. One is expected to follow a husband (today, even a lover) to another city, putting aside one's own educational and occupational plans. If a boy wants to see you, studying for an exam is supposed to be forgotten.

When a man loves a woman he says: I love you. Marry me. Bear my children. Keep the house clean. Share my professional goals. Entertain my friends and business associates. Give up your name. Give up your professional goals. Do not sleep with other men (you are my chattel). Be home when I come home from work. Because *I love you!* (One can hardly imagine what he might say if he didn't love her.)

In past centuries, woman's place was definied by economic necessity—someone had to weave the cloth, grow the food. Today our slavery is to a great extent voluntary: what keeps us in our place is the notion of love.

Lenin pointed out that in marriage, the wife is the proletariat, the husband is the bourgeois. Marriage is very good for men. Despite the message in cartoons and television "comedies," marriage does not inhibit a man in doing "his thing." It helps him. The family is his back-up crew. He gets admiration, and his meals cooked. He also has the pleasure of seeing his children for some fourteen minutes a day (this figure from a study at the University of Michigan, 1969).

The Executive Wife[5] by Ninki Hart Burger, was written to describe the role of the upper middle class woman, and to help her adjust to her situation. In the final chapter, addressed to the husbands, the author writes:

> But is the executive's wife a bystander? Or can she perform an active and constructive role in the daily drama of the backstage wife? . . . This book is confidently addressed to your wife and to a definition of her responsibilities, her relationships, her resources, and her rewards. Hopefully, each chapter may help her to help you. Happily, all the pages combined may motivate her to work to uncover a richer enjoyment for her own life, and indirectly for yours.

All the pages combined tell us much about the second sex. The women who were interviewed for this book, and to whom it is addressed, are of course the luckiest women, the richest women; they lead the lives to which all other women aspire. Thus: "As the executive works harder and climbs higher, his home denotes a place for relaxation. Not, as his wife expects, a place for partnership in marriage. The demands of the job take their toll. Domestic disaster hovers like an ominous albatross over the old homestead."

The author quotes from extensive interviews with executive wives:

"I felt so terribly lonely. I think that's why I started drinking," said the wife of an executive who had just been pictured on the cover of *Business Week*. "You see, he can lose himself in his work. And the children have lives of their own. But what do I have? Only this." And she held up a bottle of liquor.

Betty Friedan predicted several years ago that if the role of women did not change drastically in this country, the rage and hatred women feel would emerge outward —toward men. "It's horrible to discover you hate your husband," said one executive wife.[6] "And even worse, that he hates you." Sally Kempton[7] writes, "I used to lie in bed beside my husband and wish I had the courage to bash in his head with a frying pan."

The executive wife has many pleasures (notably, a lot of money) but she pays for them. Ms. Burger relates one incident where a wife was one of a party taken out to dinner by the boss. The boss suggested that everyone eat oysters, the specialty of the house. She ate them, although she had hated oysters all her life. Her husband later thanked her, and told her a horror story about some other wife who had not eaten what she was supposed to, and thereby caused her husband to lose a big contract.

"Today, it is agreed, very few men reach the top brass classification unless their wives are socially acceptable. In fact, at the annual meeting of one of the country's most powerful corporations, the chairman of the board insists that the wife of each officer sit directly behind her husband. It is his public tribute to the invaluable performance of the distaff side."[8]

It has been my observation, living for years in academic communities, that faculty wives are schooled to blend into the background. Although they are typically well-educated (most have master's degrees), they present neutral personalities: their clothing is not colorful, their conversation is quiet and undemanding. The brilliantly plumed husband, talking about political science or engineering with his colleagues, is always the star of the show.

The executive wife is given the same instructions. ". . . At the proper time, she rivets her attention to the podium, to the speaker or entertainer. She applauds discreetly at the right point. She does not distract from the guests of honor by fidgeting with her wrap or necklace. Instead of upstaging, she fades into the background."

Being anonymous has its benefits: one can lead a quiet personal life. However, the executive wife has all the liabilities of a public figure, without the ego gratification. Wives are the unpaid helpers of their husbands, and they work very hard in the executive/professional class. It is the practice in many occupations to get the wife's services free, while paying for the husband's. A man I know who directs summer camps, takes his wife along. Although she is a professional in her own right, and extremely competent, she gets no pay for the work she does. Apparently neither she nor her husband nor the employer have ever thought *she* should be paid.

Ms. Burger interviewed men who hire executives: "But supposing we're appraising her husband as the new vice president of marketing or public relations or sales. A definite stipulation is that she must accompany her husband to sales meetings or conventions or special events." This would automatically preclude the wife's working in her own profession. ". . . She may have to head up the committee to plan a week's activities for one hundred wives of salesmen or distributors. As the wife of an executive director of a trade association or the general manager of an industrial organization, her participation is one-third as vital as her husband's. She cooperates as a team. Side by side with her husband, she works late, night after night, and day after day, including weekends. It's a very special role, not unlike that of the wife of a politician or a college president."

The executive wife knows when to keep her mouth closed.

> "Husbands are not understanding. If I let my husband know how involved these parties are, what it takes out of me, and how much I'm doing, I'm in trouble. I don't know whether it makes him feel guilty or what. But he'll embarrass me by saying to our guests, 'She was out in the kitchen until 1 a.m. this morning, cooking and preparing.'
>
> "You mustn't show you're too aggressive. Spence likes to talk about me behind my back. That I'm doing things he's really proud of. I find that out from friends. But I don't confront him with anything he can label as aggressive. He just doesn't like it. I keep it buried away, separate from being a wife."

What it boils down to, is that husbands consider their wives' first job to be: wife. You may do other things, but don't let them interfere with your real job. As sociologist William Goode of Columbia University put it: "Upper class husbands are more subtle; they demand special preference in the name of their careers. . . . Studies show that executives, more than any other group of husbands, do not want their wives to work. Unexpectedly, opposition is not primarily because of a challenge to their earning power, but because they 'prefer their wives to be free to take care of their creature comforts and to provide the proper home setting for their careers.' "[9]

With any group but rich men, the wife can be imprisoned in her home for "practical" reasons. She must cook and clean—they cannot afford household help. She must care for the children twenty-four hours a day—there are no child care facilities and she cannot afford a nanny. The executives point up the true political reality: when all is said and done, the wife must be there, even if it is to *wait* for the moment when he can give her an order. I heard a man, defending his opposition to his wife's working, even though all the children were grown, say that he needed her at home when "packages were delivered."

The most frightening passage[10] in Ms. Burger's excellent book is a description of what happens to a man when he is out of work. He loses all prestige and status: he does *women's work!*

> "Remember the Gordons? Used to live in the house next to you. Louis just couldn't find another job. Same field as your husband. For months and months, he looked and looked. You know how that turned out. His wife got a job in a doctor's office. He wound up cooking, shopping, taking care of the kids. They just switched roles. He never did go back to work. Stayed home. Gave up."

"Marriage as it is now structured is great for men, but it's not really all that good for women," said Dr. Jessie Bernard, sociologist and author.[11] "More married women, as compared to single women, are depressed, passive, and phobic and show more psychosomatic symptoms. The fact that women are willing to pay this price for marriage shows they need and want it, but can't devise ways of structuring marriage which would not impose such disabilities on them. One of the discontinuities in the lives of women is the change in occupation which marriage imposes. Every wife becomes a housewife. It's been compared to a situation in which every man becomes a janitor upon marriage."

Psychoanalyst Robert Seidenberg[12] adds: "The renunciation of living asked of the wife is excessive, and leads usually to a gradual mental deterioration from sensory deprivation—a lack of contact with the participation in worldly happenings."

Since getting married is the only real success expected of a woman, she voluntarily gets herself into a situation where she will be dominated, where her identity (Mary Smith) will become Mrs. John Doe, Susie's mother. Dr. Bernard says women are willing to pay the price—depression, passivity, phobias, and psychosomatic symptoms—for marriage. Perhaps this is because there are no alternatives open to them. The single woman in America is looked down upon; none of the glamour surrounding the bachelor comes to her. She is simply a woman whom no man would "honor," would accept.

John Stuart Mill[13] said in 1869 "Marriage is the only actual bondage known to our law. There remain no legal slaves, except the mistress of every house."

It might be noted that the Greek origin of the word "idiot," *idion,* means the private life to which the women of Greece were consigned.

A recent book, *The Jewish Wife,*[14] describes well the private life to which the women of America are consigned. Although written to compare Jewish with non-Jewish housewives in order to break down many of the stereotypes of the so-called Jewish mother, the book serves also to describe the hopes, dreams, and aspirations of all middle and upper class American women.

When Schwartz and Wyden asked "What happened to you recently that gave you a big lift in morale?" many women cited weight losses, even though one of them had achieved her goal only because she had just suffered through a severe intestinal virus upset.

When asked "What have you done recently that's fun?" a wealthy woman in Scarsdale said:

"Let's see . . . I guess I'd have to say that remodelling this kitchen was a big satisfaction. I guess that's the same as fun. Anyway, I thoroughly enjoyed doing it. We used to have this white kitchen floor and it looked dirty so often that I *hated* it. Now, as you can see, I have this fabulous blue and white linoleum that looks like marble and it doesn't have to be waxed at all . . ."

These women have accepted their role, but not without rebellion. A woman who was asked about her days as a clerical worker, said: "I never learned how to change typewriter ribbons. I saw to that. In a pinch I helped out with the typing, but only in a pinch. I hate any sort of clerical work. I could never *stand* to put someone else's thoughts down on paper!"

When you cannot put your own thoughts down on paper, you look for excitement. When asked by Schwartz and Wyden whether she found the questions painful (some were quite personal), a Levittown, New York, wife replied: "I thoroughly enjoyed this interview. You can see how starved we are for diversion."

The authors of *The Jewish Wife* quoted a study which contrasted attitudes toward college for children among Jews and non-Jews. Interesting for our purposes, however, is the contrast between expectations for daughters and sons. A study of 427 mothers in 62 communities, reported by sociologist Bernard C. Rosen (in *American Sociological Review*) found that 96% of the Jewish mothers expected their sons to graduate from college, compared with 88% of the Protestant mothers and 64% of the mothers who came from Italian backgrounds. However, only 31% of the Jewish mothers had such expectations for their daughters, as compared with 25% of the non-Jews.

John Stuart Mill[15] elaborated on the theme of woman's consignment to private life: "Independently of the regular offices of life which devolve upon a woman, she is expected to have her time and faculties always at the disposal of everybody. If a man has not a profession to exempt him from such demands, still, if he has a pursuit, he offends nobody by devoting his time to it; occupation is received as a valid excuse for his not answering to every casual demand which may be made on him."

An example of this, familiar to every wife, is that when Daddy is reading the newspaper, nobody bothers him. Even when the wife and mother is doing something more creative than reading the paper, she is still expected to stop for any and every family demand. "It requires" says Mill, "an illness in the family or something else out of the common way, to entitle her to give her own business the precedence over other people's amusement. She must always be at the beck and call of somebody, generally of everybody. . . . A celebrated woman remarks that everything a woman does is done at odd times."

Mill also discusses in this connection the lack of political class consciousness of women:

> But though women do not complain of the power of husbands, each complains of her own husband, or of the husbands of her friends. It is the same in all other cases of servitude, at least in the commencement of the emancipatory movement. The serfs did not at first complain of the power of their lords, but only of their tyranny. . . . The commoners began by claiming a few municipal privileges; they next asked for an exemption for themselves from being taxed without their own consent; but they would at that time have thought it a great presumption to claim any share in the king's sovereign authority. The case of women is now the only case in which to rebel against established rules is still looked upon with the same eyes as was formerly a subject's claim to the right of rebelling against his king. A woman who joins in any movement which her husband disapproves, makes herself a martyr, without even being able to be an apostle, for the husband can legally put a stop to her apostleship.

As thorough and brilliant as Mill's insight into the female condition is, he nonetheless is male. Probably this explains his next comment; or perhaps what he says *was* true before the new militancy of the women in the 70s: "Women cannot be expected to devote themselves to the emancipation of women, until men in considerable number are prepared to join with them in the undertaking."[16]

One thing the movement has done for women in the 70s is to teach us that a) men in considerable numbers will not help us fight our battle; and b) we have the strength to fight it alone. Each woman in the movement, when interviewed, used to claim that she was married to the one perfect male, that her husband/lover was in complete agreement with the goals of female liberation, and that he helped her achieve these goals. No doubt these males exist, but most of us now feel a duty to our fellowwomen to tell the truth: there are very few liberated men, and only a liberated man can truly help us fight our battle. For this reason, women, and particularly young women, should be told that men don't dig this whole business. They have a lot of privilege, and privilege is a pleasure and hard to give up.

Moreover, most men do not understand women. Women are trained from the cradle to "understand men." This is our stock and trade. But as even the most sensitive person would not try to "understand" his butler, most men do not relate to women as human beings. Mill points out that the relations which men have with women are limited.[17]

> Many a man thinks he perfectly understands women, because he has had amatory relations with several, perhaps with many of them. If he is a good observer, and his experience extends to quality as well as quantity, he may have learnt something of one narrow department of their nature—an important department, no doubt. . . . Even with true affection, authority on the one side and subordination on the other prevent perfect confidence.

And, there is little question that male-female relations have always been those of master and servant. "By the old laws of England, the husband was called the *lord* of the wife; he was literally regarded as her sovereign, inasmuch that the murder of a man by his wife was called treason and was more cruelly avenged than was usually the case with high treason, for the penalty was burning to death. . . . If the man exerts his whole power, the woman is of course crushed: but if she is treated with indulgence, and permitted to assume power, there is no rule to set limits to her encroachments. The law, not determining her rights, but theoretically allowing her none at all, practically declares that the measure of what she has a right to, is what she can contrive to get." [18]

There is, therfore, a very real and necessary origin to the so-called feminine wiles. Women, being devoid of economic and political power, must use their sexual charm to exist at all.

> When we put together three things—first, the natural attraction between opposite sexes; secondly, the wife's entire dependence on the husband, every privilege or pleasure she has being either his gift, or depending entirely on his will; and lastly, that the principal object of human pursuit, consideration, and all objects of social ambition, can in general be sought or obtained by her only through him, it would be a miracle if the object of being attractive to men had not become the polar star of feminine education and formation of character. And, this great means of influence over the minds of women having been acquired, an instinct of selfishness made men avail themselves of it to the utmost as a means of holding women in subjection, by representing to them meekness, submissiveness, and resignation of all individual will into the hands of a man, as an essential part of sexual attractiveness. [19]

There is no question that today, with all the problems of over-population and pollution, the exclusive role of woman as brood mare is no longer necessary, and is even anti-social. Nonetheless, until recently, producing the children was the dominant role for women and determined every aspect of her destiny:

> The general opinion of men is supposed to be, that the natural vocation of a woman is that of a wife and mother. . . . I should like to hear somebody openly enunciating the doctrine—"It is necessary to society that women should marry and produce children. They will not do so unless they are compelled. Therefore, it is necessary to compel them." The merits of the case would then be clearly defined. It would be exactly that of the slave-holders of South Carolina and Louisiana—"It is necessary that cotton and sugar should be grown. White men cannot produce them. Negroes will not, for any wages which we choose to give. *Ergo* they must be compelled."[20]

One of the basic problems of women is the reconciliation of our reproductive role and our part in productive labor. Enslavement to the generative function is the fundamental fact that from the beginning has doomed women to domestic work and prevented us from taking part in the shaping of the world. Until recently there was no effective birth control; even today, it is difficult for many women to obtain satisfactory birth control devices.

In female animals, there is a physiological and seasonal rhythm that assures the economizing of their strength; in women, on the contrary, between puberty and the menopause, nature sets no limits to the number of pregnancies. Therefore, biology (the potential for continuous motherhood) combines with socio-political pressures (all women must marry), to condemn us to a single alternative as a career: wife.

Chekhov said: "If you're afraid of loneliness, don't marry." The literature on marriage (and not anti-marriage literature, at that) gives ample evidence that the problems in marriage for a woman go far beyond loneliness. In *Why Isn't a Nice Girl Like You Married*,[21] there is a section on why every girl should have more than one boyfriend at a time. The reason given is that no one man should take up your life unless you have a wedding ring. "You should never give up your privacy, your apartment, or your friends—male or female—for anything less than a Mrs."

The implication is clear: it is fine to give up your privacy, your apartment, and your friends, for a Mrs. The last is particularly telling. Every one knows that married women are not supposed to have men friends. Women I know are embarrassed to eat lunch in a public restaurant with a man who is not their husband. This is presumably because the husband or one of his friends might see his chattel lunching with another man, and become angry. The connotations here are more than sexual (since persons can easily have sexual encounters without being publicly seen); they indicate the desire of the husband to control the thoughts and actions of the wife, to choose her companions, more or less like an oversolicitious parent supervises the friends for the child.

One theory for the origin of the wedding ring is that ancient peoples, believing in magic, had the male make a cord and bind it around the waist of the woman he wanted. This was supposed to bind her to him forever. Later on, a woman would have fetters around the wrists and ankles, indicating that she had been captured and was the property of a man in the tribe. Today the wedding ring is a symbol that the woman can give up "her privacy, her apartment, and her friends—male or female." Ms. Greer clarifies:

> The freedom to have men friends is a special perogative of *single* women . . . and you should certainly take advantage of it while you can. Aside from being beneficial to your relationships with lovers and suitors, men friends are just plain fun. They're great for your ego, because compliments mean more coming from a man (especially an attractive one). Men are usually more direct and objective than women, and are thus better sounding boards

for many ideas and problems. Men also tend to have a good sense of humor, a wide variety of interests, and an intense involvement in the world—qualities which make them excellent company. All men don't have to be lovers or potential husbands; they can be interesting, entertaining, and even exciting as friends.

Until I became a conscious feminist, I could have written these words. That they might be written by a man is very understandable and not frightening: of course men should think that compliments from a man are more important to a woman than those from a woman. Of course men should think men are more direct and objective than woman, and have better senses of humor and a wide variety of interests. But highly intelligent women like Ms. Greer should not think so. The true danger of the male supremacist culture we live in is precisely that *even superior women still think men are better*. Until we can purge ourselves of this myth, we don't only have a long way to go, we have the whole way to go.

Charles Hamilton said, in a speech to the NAACP,[22] that black people can't forget for one minute what the enemy is: racism. He said that racism was the same thing whether practiced with the snarl of the South or with the smile of the North. Woman cannot forget for one minute what the enemy is: male supremacy. It is the same thing whether practiced with the snarl of the man who clomps his wife across the mouth, or with the smile of the liberal academic who explains why two Ph.D.'s are not needed in the family.

Maintaining a home, be it a hippie pad or a suburban ranch house, is a lot of work. There are several facts of life that young women should know before entering into housekeeping with a husband or lover. First of all, the society provides few services (food services, cleaning services, etc.) to make housekeeping easier. Secondly, men

THE YOUNG WOMAN'S GUIDE TO LIBERATION

do not do this kind of work. The more intelligent and educated they are, the more complex is their rationale for not doing it, but the facts are that you end up with the garbage work. If there is money available (yours, his) household help can take the burden off you. But supervising the help is your job; men do not deal with such trivia. And, on the maid's day off, it is you who fills in for her. Thirdly, if and when there are children, they are your responsibility. Men will give a variety of reasons as to why this is so, ranging from you gave birth to them, therefore you are uniquely qualified to wipe their noses for the next twenty years, to their work is too crucial socially to be interrupted for a visit to the pediatrician. Fourthly, there will be an atmosphere in the home that the male is smarter, both more practical and more theoretical, and if you fail to recognize this you have some kind of psychological problem.

Lastly, and most important, you are created for the male's pleasure. This means, if he wants sex, you want sex. If he doesn't want sex, you don't want sex. If he wants to travel, you do; if he likes the fireside, so do you. Money spent on his desires is his due: he works for it. Money spent on your desires is only made available when there is a lot of money, when you earn it yourself and *demand* to keep it for yourself, or when your "selfishness" is being indulged. (Selfishness can include such indulgence as college tuition.)

In Pearl Buck's *Command the Morning,* several wives of scientists working on the secret atomic project at Los Alamos are caught in the usual, antiquated variety of American marriage. They have the choice of living a lonely life with secretive husbands who cannot share with them the excitement of their work, or looking for some secret excitement of their own in love affairs. Only the heroine, a female physicist, is shown to have a complete life, for she shares the creative suspense of the scientists. And as she and one of the scientists become involved in work together, they inevitably fall in love. Ms. Buck is unable to conceive any outcome for this affair except a conventional home-bound marriage, or no marriage at all. And so, her female physicist rejects her lover and the prospect of imprisonment in domesticity, because she can't give up science.

"Today's Chuckle," a daily joke which appears in many newspapers in the United States, deals with male-female relations most of the time. Women are portrayed as spending too much money, talking too much, and with other common misogynist sterotypes. Recently, the chuckle was: "A man never knows how much his wife suffers. Unless, of course, he listens."[23]

An article in the *New York Times*,[24] described how legislators in Hong Kong are barring the taking of concubines. In attacking the charge that concubinage interferes with equality of the sexes, Man Kwei-chi, special councilor of the executive committee, said it all. "There is no such thing. A woman takes on the name of the man she marries, and besides, the first human beings to set foot on the moon were men."

NOTES TO CHAPTER X

1. Gilman, Charlotte Perkins. *Women and Economics.* New York: Charlton, 1898.
2. *Ibid.*
3. "Are Women Human Beings? A Consideration of the Major Error in the Discussion of Women Suffrage," *Harper's Weekly,* May 25, 1912, p. 11.
4. Auchincloss, Louis. *World of Profit.* Boston: Houghton Mufflin Company, 1968, p. 92
5. Burger, Ninki Hart. *The Executive Wife.* New York: The Macmillan Company, 1968.
6. *Ibid.* p. 62.
7. *Esquire,* July, 1970.
8. Burger, *op. cit.* p. 119.
9. *Ibid.* p. 249.
10. *Ibid.,* p. 173.
11. At the 61st annual meeting of the American Home Economics Association, June 24, 1970.
12. Seidenberg, *op. cit.*
13. Mill, John Stuart. *"The Subjection of Women," Three Essays.* London: Oxford University Press, 1912, Chapter IV.
14. Gwen Gibson Schwartz and Barbara Wyden. *The Jewish Wife.* New York: Peter H. Wyden, Inc., Publisher, 1969.
15. Mill, *op. cit.,* Chapter III.
16. *Ibid.*
17. *Ibid.*
18. *Ibid.,* Chapter II.
19. *Ibid.*
20. *Ibid.*
21. Greer, Rebecca E. *Why Isn't a Nice Girl Like You Married.* New York: The Macmillan Company, 1969, p. 104.
22. July 2, 1970.
23. April 21, 1970.
24. May 30, 1970.

CHAPTER XI

All Ye Need to Know:
Beauty Is Truth

Beauty is truth, truth beauty,—that is all
Ye know on earth, and all ye need to know.
John Keats, "Ode on a Grecian Urn," Stanza 5

*H*UGH HEFNER was on one of the talk shows recently[1] discussing the changing policies at Playboy magazine. Until this year, he said, they had not allowed the Playmate of the Month to increase her breast size with silicone. The feeling of the editorial board had been that they wanted "real" women. However, this year they changed their policy. They realized that siliconing the breast is a cosmetic change, available to and used by women to make themselves more beautiful. It is no different than having one's nose bobbed, having one's ears pinned back, having one's hair straightened, having one's face lifted, having one's ears pierced, having one's toes removed to fit pointed shoes (some California women did it a few years ago), having one's face sandpapered, or wearing makeup. With this realization, the editorial board of Playboy opened the opportunity to become the Playmate of the Month to girls not naturally endowed with enormous breasts. Whereas last year Hefner and staff were turning away women who used silicone; this year they had agreed to "accept" it.

Cynthia Goodings, the Playmate of the Year, was asked why she posed for the center fold. She replied, "for money."

A nightclub in Syracuse, New York, features as cocktail waitresses what they call Little Foxes (the central New York answer to the Playboy Club). The Little Foxes wear costumes which aim to make the waitress look as busty as possible. If she is small busted, the costume pushes her breasts up, so that it looks like she really has a lot of cleavage. In June 1970; one of the Little Foxes, Mary Chamberlain, who had served drinks for months in a satisfactory manner, was fired on the spot when a Holiday Inn executive noticed her in her street clothes and realized she was totally flat-chested. She was, he claimed, ruining "their image."

Interesting though this incident is to illustrate the oppression of women and to highlight our role as sex objects, a male reaction to it is more interesting still. I told the Little Fox tale to a man I know, a man with a high IQ and with a great social conscience—*i.e.*, he understands how the exploitation of black people has affected them. His reaction was: we need have no pity for this woman. She exploited her own sexiness to earn money. This reaction illustrates the inability of most men, even intelligent, sensitive ones, to recognize:

1. Women's economic plight. (We cannot earn money.)
2. Our need to exploit sexiness to eat. (Little Foxes trade big breasts for tips. Wives trade sex for food.)

3. The fact that exploiting sexiness pays much better than filing cards. (The Little Fox earns about $40 a night. The file clerk earns about $15 for a whole day's work.)

When parents gaze in awe at a new baby boy, they think: he may some day be President of the United States. When parents gaze in awe at a new baby girl, they think: she may some day be Miss America.

Miss America does indeed represent the ideal American woman. Whereas Playmate of the Month may meet with embarrassment in some of the more puritanical sections of the country, Miss America is the female American dream. She is, in one person, beautiful, mindless, passive, and *a consumer*. (She spends her entire year as reigning queen traveling around the country advertising products.)

On August 22, 1968, a women's liberation group issued a release which announced perhaps the most famous action of the movement. The release read:

NO MORE MISS AMERICA!

> On September 7th in Atlantic City, the Annual Miss America Pageant will again crown "your ideal." But this year, reality will liberate the contest auction-block in the guise of 'genyooine' de-plasticized, breathing women. . . . We will protest the image of Miss America, an image that oppresses women in every area in which it purports to represent us. There will be: Picket Lines; Guerrilla Theater; Leafleting; Lobbying Visits to the contestants urging our sisters to reject the Pageant farce and join us; a huge Freedom Trash Can (into which we will throw bras, girdles, curlers, false eyelashes, wigs, and representative issues of *Cosmopolitan, Ladies' Home Journal, Family Circle,* etc.—bring any such woman-garbage you have around the house). . . . It should be a groovy day on the Boardwalk in the sun with our sisters. . . . *We will reclaim ourselves for ourselves.* On to Atlantic City!

Miss America and Playmate of the Month are sisters under the skin. To win approval, we must be both sexy and wholesome ("her favorite sports are swimming and tennis"), delicate but able to cope (with Bert Parks' questions about American foreign policy). Deviation from this ideal may bring disaster: You won't get a man.

Women in our society are forced daily to compete for male approval. We are enslaved by ludicrous "beauty" standards. If we could learn to accept these standards as "what the Man wants," it would not be so demeaning. (I must earn money and the qualifications here are big breasts, or sweet smiles, or whatever.) The tragedy is that women accept these standards as their own. We judge ourselves and our sisters by these standards. The unattractive girl is not only looked down upon by the male, she is looked down upon by her sisters. Self-hate has taken its final toll.

Men are judged by their actions; women by their appearance. A man once seriously asked me if plastic surgeons can do anything about a square face. (I have a square face.) The idea was that I would be more beautiful if I could have my jaw broken and reset.

Women not only must be beautiful, we must be young. While perhaps pleasant news for the young woman (she has a natural advantage over older women), it is basically bad news even for the teenager. First of all, we all know that we will grow old. While there is general anguish in the human condition itself—all people know they will die—there is specific anguish in the female condition—because females know that in a very real sense they will die at twenty-one. The thirtieth birthday party is supposed to be a day of sorrow for a woman: if she isn't married, even her most "optimistic" relative has given up by this time; if she is married, she must now start her twenty-year vigil to keep her husband away from the "pretty young girls." If she cannot succeed (and we know that many a forty year old executive "turns in" his wife for a younger model), she loses her social position, and often (the tales of giant alimony settlements to the contrary) her source of income.

Marjorie Morningstar is a novel about a wealthy young girl, growing up in the suburbs of New York. She has incorporated well the standards of her family and the society: she knows she is young and beautiful, but will be neither for very long, and hence, must catch the right man—and keep him. The Morningstar syndrome affects every young girl growing up. When I was in college there was a myth going around the "all the good boys are gone by the time you are seniors." This meant, of course, that one must recognize that one is a "morningstar" and get married, or at least engaged, before age twenty-one. No woman is developed by twenty-one; early marriage is probably the surest way one can devise to *insure* that a woman will not develop an autonomous personality and an important career. The driving force behind early marriage is indeed the youth and beauty cult. If a woman is to be valued primarily for her youth and beauty, she cannot wait to marry until thirty. She must cash her chips while she still has them.

Women are starting to break down these myths. They will never be completely destroyed until we can earn our own living (and are not dependent upon men to support us), but the recognition of this as nonsense is a step toward freedom.

Wendy Dascomb, Miss U.S.A. 1969, told reporters that when she entered the contest, she didn't know what she was getting into.[2] "You're an animal and everybody's staring at you up and down and back up again." After a year of traveling the country in her role as Miss U.S.A., Miss Dascomb said: "In interviews the press always asked me the same questions. How could I be enthusiastic when I knew the fifteen questions they were going to ask?

Finally I found out they were given a list of subjects not to touch—religion, politics and the pill. These are my favorite subjects to talk about. I hate war, and I have definite opinions on religion. It just irritates me to have to be sweet, smiling and pleasant all day. It all boils down be being a phony. The travel is great, but it wasn't much fun last fall to pose for the sponsors—like spark plugs and antifreeze. . . . And I know now I never want to become a model or a starlet." Miss Dascomb is a college freshman who plans to be a special education teacher.

Selling spark plugs and antifreeze is no fun. Only a small segment of the female population is "beautiful" enough to sell products. But we can all—old and young, unattractive and pretty—*buy*. Women buy cosmetics from age twelve on. The older we get, the more we buy, because all the ads promise that the product will make us young.

Women buy a lot when they are single, but they buy more when they are married. One of the seriously-given objections to men and women living together without being married is that they do not set up elaborate households. They do not buy the incredible amounts of unnecessary junk which the average American couple thinks necessary for comfortable living.

Betty Friedan upset Wall Street in 1963 with her analysis of the sexual sell[3]:

> Why is it never said that the really crucial function, the really important role that women serve as housewives is *to buy more things for the house.* In all the talk of femininity and woman's role, one forgets that the real business of America is business. But the perpetuation of housewifery, the growth of the feminine mystique, makes sense (and dollars) when one realizes that women are the chief customers of American business. Somehow, somewhere, someone must have figured out that women will buy more things if they are kept in the underused, nameless-yearning, energy-to-get-rid-of state of being housewives.

We must buy floor wax, and we must buy cosmetics. Beauty is a big business. Buying more things for the face and body is a big business. We have been so bludgeoned into thinking that our success in life is dependent on catching and keeping a man—and that the way to do this is to be beautiful—and that the way to be beautiful is to look like a Hollywood starlet—that the cosmetics industry, to name only one, is making millions and millions of dollars on us each year, selling products which cost pennies to produce and which in the final analysis do little or nothing for our happiness.

I would suggest that one of the ways that the cosmetics industry could make reparations to the women of America would be to establish scholarships and fellowship funds for us, to enable us to improve our minds and not our eyelashes.

In 1967, over $500 million was spent on cosmetics advertising.[4] This gives some idea of the profits which are being made on women each year. A National Educational Television (NET) program, shown November 1, 1967, "On Face Value," described how a beauty product selling for 50¢ is automatically scorned by most women who think that they are not obtaining quality merchandise. Dermatologists indicated that soap and water and perhaps one cream would probably suffice for most women, but they also pointed out that a pound of cream costing perhaps 32¢ could be successfully retailed for $5. "The illusive ingredient making possible such a whopping mark-up, is eternal feminine hope."

What are we hoping for? We are hoping for a man. Notice a few magazine article titles, and think of how ludicrous it would be to have such reading matter in men's magazines, for men. "Are you ready to be seen?" (Ladies Home Journal); "Basic beauty course for girls" (Senior Scholastic—think of the Senior Scholastic running an article entitled Basic beauty course for boys!); "Beauty stop-over: Linda Roy, winner in the Westinghouse science talent search" *(Seventeen)*; "Big beauty debate: husbands vs. bachelors: ideas of what constitutes a really good-looking woman" *(McCalls)*; "Crash beauty: crash course in beauty at the U. of Pennsylvania *(Mademoiselle—*is that also what the boys at the U. of Pennsylvania study?); "For your most romantic party look: ribbons, ringlets and radiance" *(Good Housekeeping)*; "How to stay young" *(Ladies Home Journal*; "$750 worth of beauty advice from fifteen experts" *(Ladies Home Journal)*; "Stay young and beautiful" *(Parents Magazine)*.

The very young woman (with usually neither husband nor career to give her self-confidence) is particularly attack-able by the beauty sell. "Mass media today both promotes and capitalizes on this vulnerability of the teen-age girls. Products are designed and advertised to cash in on the societal imperative. The commercial always describes beauty as the aim and marriage as the goal. A literal flesh market is created where one's destiny is determined on whether one smells right or whether one's hair is straight and without dandruff."[5]

Mama Portnoy may have nagged her son to stand up straight, but everyone knows that it is the girls who must be beautiful, shapely, and clean. A male simply need exist, and he is desirable. The beauty tips to females, in magazines and books, describe beautifying parts of the body which the typical woman does not even know she has. We are led on a lifelong chase, searching out the one beauty product that will "keep him forever en-chanted." We are instructed never to let him see us un-prepared: put on your false eyelashes before breakfast. We are told boys don't make passes at girls who wear glasses: why do you have to see anyway, except for gazing into his eyes?

The idiocy of all this is obvious. First of all, it turns every female human being into an object; what is appropriate for a woman who wants to go on the stage (and who is, incidentally, born with classic features) is a big waste of time for other women. Secondly, any woman who spends all day making her self beautiful will have a dull and uninteresting life because she will have little time to do anything else. Many women sleep huge portions of their day in order to avoid, so they think, the wrinkling process. And last of all, this preparation for the marriage market is a symptom of the grossest and most dangerous form of self-hate. Any human being who values herself will not spend thousands of hours and thousands of dollars to change the texture of an elbow, to alter the color of the hair, to narrow the width of an ankle. And she certainly will not undergo major surgey to pin back ears, to shorten a nose, to enlarge breasts.

Every city in the United States will soon have a Freedom Trash Can into which we can toss these expensive, painful, and degrading objects. That receptacle arrives 6,000 years late, but not too late.

Thorstein Veblen pointed out[6] at the turn of the century the marked similarity between the apparel of women and that of domestic servants. This is in contrast to the apparel (and role) of the men in the household.

> Her [the wife's] sphere is within the household, which she should "beautify", and of which she should be the "chief ornament." The male head of the household is not currently spoken of as its ornament.
>
> . . . the general disregard of the wearer's comfort which is an obvious feature of all civilized women's apparel, are so many items of evidence to the effect that in the modern civilized scheme of life the woman is still, in theory, the economic dependent of the man—that, perhaps in a highly idealized sense, she still is the man's chattel. The homely reason for all this conspicuous leisure and

attire on the part of women lies in the fact that they are servants to whom, in the differentiation of economic functions, have been delegated the office of putting in evidence their master's ability to pay.

. . . In both [women and servants] there is a very elaborate show of unnecessary expensiveness, and in both cases there is also a notable disregard of the physical comfort of the wearer. But the attire of the lady goes farther in its elaborate insistence on the idleness, if not on the physical infirmity of the wearer, than does that of the domestic. And this is as it should be; for in theory, according to the ideal scheme of the pecuniary culture, the lady of the house is the chief menial of the household.

NOTES TO CHAPTER XI

1. Dick Cavett Show, May 26, 1970.
2. Reported in *Miami Herald*, April 26, 1970. Article by Helen Vollmar.
3. Friedan, Betty. *The Feminine Mystique*. New York: W. W. Norton & Company, Inc. This from p. 197 of the Dell paperback.
4. *New York Times*, Nov. 2, 1967, p. 95.
5. Seidenberg, Robert. "The Case of the Missing Mind: Feminine Sexuality and the Adolescent Identity," *Nickel Review*, May 18, 1970.
6. Veblen, Thorstein. *Theory of the Leisure Class*, 1899. This quote from the New York edition, p. 127.

CONCLUSION

The Outer World
Is Where the Fun Is

The *power* of earning is essential to the dignity of a
woman, if she has not independent property.
John Stuart Mill, *The Subjection of Women*, 1869

Women are in slavery because of economic dependence.
Charlotte Perkins Gilman, *Women and Economics*, 1898.

WOMEN LACK POLITICAL POWER. Women suffer from
lack of self-love. But perhaps the real key to our problem
is that we *don't have money*. This lack of green power occurs first of all because we are trained from birth not to
aspire to the well-paying jobs in the society. Secondly,
even those of us who do, are kept from those positions
by hundreds of spoken and unspoken barriers.

Critics of women's equality often say that men are
"destroyed" when they lose their jobs whereas women
are not. The answer to that is of course that given the
pay and interest value of most of our jobs, no one could
be destroyed to lose them.

All women are poor. We are supported by our husbands, our lovers, or our fathers. To keep this support
we must do more or less what they expect us to do, or

the money will be withdrawn. If we are not supported by men, we are (poorly) supported by the (male-run) government, via the welfare system. In addition to being conditioned not to work, or not to work at lucrative jobs, we are kept out of the higher-paying occupations with systematic rigor. We are not hired for good jobs, we are paid less for the same work, and we are not promoted. All this is illegal, under Title VII of the Civil Rights Act of 1964 and under the Equal Pay Act of 1963. Men not only earn more money, but since 1955 the gap has been steadily widening. In 1955, the average American woman who worked full time earned $63.00 for each $100 earned by the average American man. By 1968, we earned only $58.20 for each $100 earned by a man.

Betty Friedan emphasized at the Fourth National Conference of the National Organization for Women[1] that "It is only young girls who have always been supported by Daddy who temporarily fail to understand that in a society where everything costs money, if they are not able to earn the money needed to live they will be more dependent on men, on husbands, on welfare or alimony, than their grandmothers."

One myth we often hear is that women have all the money. This is utter nonsense. Although we own half of the stock, we control hardly any of it. (It is in companies which are exclusively owned, run, and controlled by men.) The "rich widows" have their stock in the control of their male bankers, male stockbrokers, or sons.

In 1968, when the *Harvard Business Review* wanted to do a study of women executives, the editors were forced to conclude that there was no one to study. American business, like every other institution in the country, is totally controlled by men.

Even in the industries where the overwhelming number of workers are female, the men make more money.

In New York City, 75% of the garment workers are women; we earn $2.24 per hour, as compared to $3.27 per hour for men.

In the "men's professions" the situation is much worse. Female law school graduates earn 40% less than their male peers the first year out of school. (Only 3% of the lawyers in the country are female.) After ten years in the profession, we earn 500% less. Women chemists earn $4500 a year less than men.

Our position in the world of employment is, along with black people, that of nigger. We are the last hired, the first fired. We do the most uninteresting, dirty work. And, although no one dares to utter such absurdity today about black people, we are supposed to *enjoy* giving service.

Women are a reserve army of labor to bring wages down. For example, we have been used during a time of war to take the place of male workers needed by the military. Often, we have been used against collectively organized groups of workers, since our condition forces us to work for lower pay.

Women's work is not taken seriously. Anthropologists have found this to be a universal phenomenon. For example, in a tribe where women make the pottery and men do the fishing, the fishing is the status job. In a tribe where women do the fishing and men make the pottery, the potter has the top position. When a husband works at home, the duty of the wife is to keep the children and herself silent, so he can go ahead with his creative production. When a wife works at home, there is no attempt to assist her. Moreover, she is typically "on call" to meet anyone's needs—which may simply mean her husband feels like chatting. The implication in the home is that if a member of the family needs something, the woman should take care of it. If she has enough gall to write instead of cook, that should be sacrifice enough on the part of the family.

A good example of this is seen in student life. Married male students, undergraduate and graduate, usually have working wives. The student is the chosen person; family life is organized so that he can study. The women do the housework and take care of the children—or make provisions for child care, which is almost impossible, given the lack of child care facilities in our society. (Every man has them—a wife; women do not have them.) Wives of students also do research, typing, and editing, in addition to cooking, laundry, and cleaning, and of course, working at their own jobs. Married female students usually have working husbands. But here the parallel ends. Although burdened with studying, they also do all the housework, cooking, shopping, laundry. They also type their own papers, do their own research. The greatest contrast beween the male and female student mates, however, is not in the actual work done to help a student get through school: it is in the *attitude*. Wives of students regard their husbands with awe—they join the Law Wives, they even get PhT degrees ("Putting Hubby Through"). Husbands of students usually regard their wives as being somewhat frivolous. They often consider themselves very generous indeed to "allow" their wives to pursue higher education; many actively fight their wives' going to school. And even those who are in agreement with the plan do not consider it their duty, for example, to make dinner while exams are going on.

It is in countries that are either highly socialized (with communal day nurseries, like Russia) or underdeveloped (with a large lower class from which to draw household help, like India) that women professionals can thrive. In addition to having the almost insurmountable child care problem, the American working wife must face the income tax laws which are not structured for working women. She may deduct only up to $600 a year for baby-sitting fees—up to $900 for two or more children—but only if the combined income of husband and wife is *less than $5,000.*

One can tell much about what a society values by looking at the tax structure. In America we reward people for getting married, for having children, for buying homes, and for leaving the inner city for the suburbs. We punish them for staying single, for not breeding, and for renting apartments. The social security and tax laws are designed to punish the working wife. The only return in future Social Security retirement benefits which the 12,500,000 American working wives will get is the difference between the benefits one can expect as a dependent wife and the amount of her own benefit, based on contributions to the system. When the Social Security law was written in the 30s, the vast majority of wives were nonworking wives and totally dependent on their husbands' incomes—and thus, also retirement benefits—for economic survival.[2] The basic principle was, and it remains, that the husband is the key breadwinner of the family. The supplement for his non-working wife was put into the law to keep millions of retired married couples off the welfare roles.

As of December 1967, the working wife represented 57% of the female labor force. Today, the married woman now outnumbers the single woman in the work force by 2.5 to 1. The wife who works is contributing *billions* of dollars to Social Security taxes to finance the benefits of someone else.

The U.S. Census refuses to recognize women as possible "heads of the household." The form asks for "Head," and "Wife of Head." There is an almost universal assumption, put forward by male social scientists, that female heads of the household spell disaster. Instead of giving high praise, for example, to the black woman, who has for so long worked and kept her family together despite fantastic odds, we read everywhere how dangerous the black woman is to her man and how having a woman as head of the household is destuctive to the children's "normal" development. This whole concept, as Constance Timberlake, an urban affairs specialist, has pointed out, is a product of the white male chauvinist mind, a theory evolved by male social scientists and propagated by the male-run press.

A question frequently asked married professional women is, what would happen if you earned more than your husband? The implication is that some dreadful result would occur. No one ever asks a married professional man, what would happen if you earned more than your wife? The message we are all supposed to have picked up as children is that the male will earn more and that any other pattern is unnatural. This is just about as dysfunctional (for individuals, for the society) a monetary caste system as one whereby blue-eyed people cannot earn more than brown-eyed ones.

Over 80% of the American poor, by government standards, are women. In addition, welfare and poverty programs discriminate against women. When the mass media refers to high school dropouts, this usually means male high school dropouts. The programs keyed to this group are for young men. The job corps prepares a small percent of females for the labor force; invariably the courses for women are in female caste jobs—hairdressers, cooks, nurses' aids.

The latest figures available[3] show that there is indeed a double standard of pay for men and women. The national averages of annual wages for full-time, year-round workers, in 1968 show:

	MEN	WOMEN
Professional & Technical Workers (Doctors, Lawyers, Scientists Draftsmen)	$10,151	$6,691
Non-Farm Managers, Officials and Proprietors (Office Managers Local, State and Federal Government Officials, Business Owners)	$10,340	$5,635
Clerical Workers (Bookkeepers, File Clerks, Stenographers)	$7,351	$4,789
Operatives (Factory Workers)	$6,738	$3,991
Service Workers (Excludes Private Household Workers; Includes Laundry Workers, Barbers, Beauty Operators)	$6,058	$3,332
Salesworkers	$8,549	$3,461

The salary difference obviously varies by occupation. The biggest discrepancy in major occupational groups is among sales workers, men earning two and a half times more than women. The smallest discrepancy is among professional and technical workers, but even there a woman's salary is only two-thirds that of a man's.

U.S. News & World Report conducted a survey on women and employment in the United States, reported April 13, 1970. They asked "what do women want?" They found: "Cold cash is one important answer. American women are up in arms over what they regard as intolerable economic discrimination against them. In industry, in government, and in the professions, women charge that they are hired last, paid least, passed over for promotion, held to the drudgery of routine jobs."

The *U.S. News* survey found that these charges are correct.

A main reason for the disparity in earnings between men and women is a difference in the jobs they are likely to hold. More that 64% of the 31.1 million women in the labor force are employed as clerical, service and sales workers, or as domestic servants—all relatively low-paying jobs. (This of course completely excludes the work which almost all women do, domestic service in their own homes which is *totally unpaid.*) About 70% of the men are employed as professional and technical workers, managers, proprietors, craftsmen, foremen or factory workers—jobs which pay better.

Men also traditionally have held most of the jobs where overtime pay is common. In many states, women have long been limited by so-called protective legislation to an eight-hour day. Most states also have had laws barring women from jobs requiring the lifting of heavy weights. These laws are being overturned in court on the grounds that they are contrary to the Civil Rights Act of 1964, Title VII, and indeed contrary to the Equal Protection Clause of the Fourteenth Amendment to the Constitution. However, hundreds of such laws still exist.

Women also are more vulnerable to unemployment than men, and this vulnerability has been increasing over the years. In 1960, the unemployment rates for men and women were nearly the same. Of the male labor force, 5.4% was unemployed; of the female labor force, 5.9%. In 1969, whereas the unemployment rate had gone down, the rate for women was twice that for men, 4.7% vs. 2.8%.

And the UPI reported that "Unemployment edged back up to 5% of the labor force in July [1970] mainly because of the inability of white women and young men re-entering the labor force to get jobs. . . . The July increase in unemployment occurred almost entirely among adult women and young adult men."

Few women have been able to enter the professions. Only 1% of the federal judges appointed by the President are women. One 1% of the engineers, 3% of the lawyers, 7% of the doctors, and 9% of the scientists are women. Even in the teaching field, traditionally female, only 19% of the college-level faculties are made up of women, although thirty years ago the figure was 30%. And these 19% are at the lowest levels of the academic hierarchy.

Women earn less than men in all kinds of jobs. The U.S. Department of Labor, National Science Foundation, found this data for 1968. Median annual earnings of full-time workers.

OCCUPATION	MEN	WOMEN
Scientists	$13,200	$10,000
Professional, technical	$10,151	$ 6,691
Proprietors, managers	$10,340	$ 5,635
Clerical workers	$ 7,351	$ 4,789
Sales workers	$. 8,549	$ 3,461
Craftsmen	$ 7,978	$ 4,625
Factory workers	$ 6,738	$ 3,991
Service workers	$ 6,058	$ 3,332

We not only earn less money at every kind of job; many of us seem completely adjusted to doing so. A survey was recently made among the 181,000 members of the National Federation of Business and Professional Women's Clubs, whose members averaged fifty to sixty years old, and so might be presumed to be well along in their careers. Their average income was $5,000–$8,000. Typically, the members owned a house and a car, and no other real estate. Their characteristic job: bookkeeper, accountant, secretary, teacher.

Studies made by the U.S. Women's Bureau show that we work because we need the money. Money was found to motivate most of the 6.5 million single-women workers. Nearly all of the 5.8 million women workers who are divorced, widowed, or separated from their husbands were found to be working for "compelling economic reasons." In addition, the 4.8 million married women whose husbands earned less than $5,000 per year were presumed to be working because they needed the money very badly.

There are persistent myths about female employment. One is that we quit working when we get married. Actually, 60% of the female labor force consists of married women whose husbands are present in the home. And, of the married working women, over half of us have children under eighteen years old. Twenty-five percent of women with children under age three are in the labor force; one-third of mothers with children in school are working. The greatest increase in working women has been among those who are married and have children.

If our poverty exists while we are working, it really exists if we are not. In 1966, 40% of adult women had *no independent income at all.* The other 60% had incomes from investments, welfare payments, earnings, and alimony, but *half of these* received less than $1,638 during the year.

Men own the railroads. Women clean up the cars. Men own the cosmetics companies. Women paint their faces. Men dominate the top ranks in the professions of cooking, dressmaking, and child study. The higher prestige and money a job carries, the fewer women who will occupy these positions. Caroline Bird[4] cites the federal government as an example of a sexist employer: ". . . the Federal Service, which employs 650,000 women, promotes them according to explicit rules, and grades the many different occupations in the Government by income brackets. In 1966, women dominated the lower grades, but they thinned out at every rise in grade until they were only 1½% of those earning $20,000 or more."

Government heads, business executives, and union leaders share equally in the discrimination to women workers. Many persons think the situation is not necessarily based on a deliberate plot, but may stem from a combination of adherence to custom, and the unfortunate fact that the number of good jobs in America is limited. There is not so much room at the top, and the white male who is up there knows it!

When statisticians from a life insurance company were studying the life expectancy of people in *Who's Who in America*, as contrasted to people not in *Who's Who*, they excluded women, "because there were too few females listed for statistical analysis."[5]

Is life for women going to continue to be as grim? Absolutely not. Ireland's Man of the Year is Bernadette Devlin. According to Valentina Nikolayeva-Tereshkova, the first women cosmonaut, women adapt to weightlessness faster than men. Ms. Tereshkova, who spent three days in space in 1963, writes in a UNESCO magazine: "A woman's flight into space produced the evidence to show that the organism of a woman can cope with all space flight factors no worse than that of a man." At present, the United States has 59 astronauts, all male. The USSR has five female cosmonauts.

Women more and more will feel no need to even justify that we are as good as men, as capable of going into space, of doing anything. We will simply demand our right to do so, and let the burden of proof be on the other side—to prove that we cannot.

The first female aquanauts completed their highly successful mission in July, 1970. It should be pointed out that last year when the Navy Department was questioned about the possibility of sending women undersea, their response was that the male aquanauts might indeed "get lonely," but that women probably couldn't adjust to the rigors of undersea life.

Two Japanese women have climbed Mt. Annapurna, in the Himalayas. The United States Army has appointed two women generals (June 1970). A woman scientist has finally been awarded an Atomic Energy Citation (July 1970). Women in Miami have applied to start the First Women's Bank of Florida. (May 1970). Bernice Gera, of Jackson Heights, New York, has won the first job as an umpire in organized baseball. And, despite the recorded (and hilarious) comments of male jockeys, women jockeys are now riding successfully all over the country.

The U.S. Forest Service has hired the first all-girl logging crew, who report: "We're in it for the money."[6] The U.S. Air Force has commissioned its first flying nun, Sister Nancy Eagen; Sister Eleanor Niedwcik, the only nun-policewoman in the country, works in Washington, D.C., and doesn't mind being referred to as "the fuzz."[7]

The Women's Heritage Series, Inc., formed by Virginia Carabillo in Los Angeles, is a new firm, devoted solely "to the creation and merchandising of products for liberated women by liberated women."

There are many occupations that are not now open to women simply because women have never been in them, and none of us has battled down the door in the particular field. Women are discriminated against, illegally, in sales jobs. With the exception of "Avon ladies," most companies do not hire door-to-door saleswomen; this goes against all logic, since housewives would be more likely to open the door to another woman. Being a college traveler for a book publisher is another lucrative field so far closed to us. Being a "detail man" who sells drugs and medical products to doctors is another. One firm which interviewed in Syracuse, New York, for traveling salesmen for a *substitute for mother's milk* refused to interview women for the job.

What about the status of women in food service? Are we admitted to the executive suite, or are we still relegated to waiting on tables? Walter Hiller, personnel director of Howard Johnson Co., waxed eloquent[8] about women waitresses, but had to be "prodded into talking about more responsible jobs for women."

At Howard Johnson's, the service and food supervisors report to the area manager—all of whom are men. Hiller initially laughed at the suggestion of a woman in that job and then reluctantly replied that it was a good one. "More men than women will work the necessary six-day week." (However, all Howard Johnson waitresses are women and they all work a six-day week.) Hiller said that "when women meet our standards, we're glad to hire them. True, a few years ago, we didn't feel this way, but the women's liberation movement has brought equality to light."

What is success, even limited success, doing for American women?[7] Making us feel just fine.

Sally Kellerman, who played Nurse Hot Lips Houlihan in MASH, reported to *Time* magazine[9] on how she feels being a star in a successful movie. "Even my analyst said it did more for me than a man could."

Many changes are necessary in this society before we can achieve full equality. But we should not wait until they are made before demanding our equality, before *taking* our liberation. We must free women from having the exclusive role in child-rearing. The word "motherhood" should be eliminated from the language—changed to "parenthood." Free child care facilities must be available 24 hours a day, for use of all parents when so desired. The role of the father must be upgraded. It may be difficult to convince some people that it is better for a child (cognitively, affectively) to be with other children, rather than cooped up with only one person all day, but it is true.

Given the population explosion and the problems of ecology, it should not be too difficult to convince women that bearing more than two children is a *disservice* to society. At the moment, the alternatives are so few that many women suffer from the Pumpkin Eater syndrome (needing to be pregnant or nursing a baby at all times to feel worthy). Bruno Bettelheim discusses how such mothers affect their children: ". . . And sadly enough the modern mother is often in a poor position to give support when her child is doing badly in school or is not very popular and hence feels defeated. Having invested so much emotionally in her child's achievement her pride suffers at his failure and as likely as not she administers a bawling out when understanding and compassion are needed."

The Canadian government gives a male employee a holiday with pay when his child is born, but a woman must give birth on her own time. Although a male in the civil service receives a day off with pay when his child is born, there is no paid maternity leave for women.[10]

In countries, and at times when women are needed out of the home, solutions are made to the child tending, cooking, cleaning problems. During World War II, child care centers sprung up all over the United States, because women were needed to work in the factories and offices. When the men returned from the war, and wanted their jobs back, the child care facilities were closed (and thousands of women were fired on the spot). Today, there are methods of cooking and cleaning that are truly time-saving, but they have not been put on the market. On the contrary, we are presented, by the male business establishment, with seven different kinds of polishes with which to clean a table. American technology has not had the incentive to work as hard at getting women out of the house as it has at getting men on the moon.

In the Scandinavian countries, in the Soviet Union, there are food and cleaning services available to families which have no full-time domestic worker (wife) in the home. In the United States, we read articles every day on how to make your own pasta from scratch, on why home-made cookies make your child happier, on how to assure yourself that American technology will never free *you* from your job as domestic.

No other society in history has had quite the set-up we have for child-rearing: the mother and child closeted up together for years. It is harmful to the child, it is harmful to the mother.

Dr. Issac Asimov writes of a happier society in 1991[11]: "The two freedoms, economic and sexual, will reinforce each other. The young lady of 1991 will not need to sell herself to any man because that is the only legal and respectable way of having sex and children; or because that is the only socially acceptable way of achieving economic security. . . . This does not necessarily mean the end of the family as an institution. It does mean the end of the family as a prison."

I have not meant to imply that women's having economic independence will mean utopia. I do mean, however, that an end to the repression of women—economic, political, psychological—will produce perhaps the most humane and far-reaching revolution in history.

Is this book a cry to revolution?

Yes.

To whom is it directed?

To all women.

Stop waiting on the men in your life: boyfriends, husbands, bosses.

Stop voting for male politicians.

Stop buying products—soap powder, dresses, eye shadow—from companies owned and controlled by men.

Stop buying messages—in newspapers, in magazines, on television—that are written and controlled by men.

Think twice about going to a church that refuses to ordain women.

Leave the baby in Daddy's office.

And don't raise your daughter to bow and scrape, to genuflect, to obey.

Genuflecting is no fun at all.

You have absolutely nothing to lose but your poverty, your neurosis, and your obedience.

NOTES TO THE CONCLUSION

1. Chicago, Illinois, March 1970.
2. A sad chapter in the history of women in America contains the fact that during the Depression married women were sweepingly fired from their jobs, in private industry and with the government. The "rationale" behind all this was that in a period where jobs were so scarce, no family should have two job-holders. The effect of this was to make women even *more* dependent upon men, economically and psychologically.
3. Department of Labor, Women's Bureau, 1970.
4. Bird, Caroline. *Born Female: The High Cost of Keeping Women Down.* New York: David McKay Company, 1968.
5. *New York Times,* July 26, 1970.
6. Associated Press, July 1, 1970.
7. United Press International, June 28, 1970.
8. *Miami Herald,* August 9, 1970. Article by Virginia Heffington.
9. *Time,* July 13, 1970.
10. *New York Times,* July 5, 1970.
11. Asimov, Issac. "Miss 1991: A New World," *Tropic* magazine, April 12, 1970.

Bibliography

Bird, Caroline. *Born Female: The High Cost of Keeping Women Down.* New York: David McKay Company, 1968.

Culver, Elsie Thomas. *Women in the World of Religion.* Garden City, New York: Doubleday & Company, 1967.

DeBeauvoir, Simone. *The Second Sex.* Translated and edited by H. M. Parshley. New York, New York: Knopf, 1953.

Ellmann, Mary. *Thinking About Women.* New York: Harcourt, Brace & World, 1968.

Engels, Friedrich. *The Origins of the Family, Private Property and the State* (1884). Translated by Ernest Untermann. Chicago: Charles Kerr, 1902.

Flexner, Eleanor. *Century of Struggle: The Woman's Rights Movement in the United States.* Cambridge, Mass., 1959.

Friedan, Betty. *The Feminine Mystique.* New York: W. W. Norton & Co., 1963.

Gilman, Charlotte Perkins. *Women and Economics.* New York: Charlton, 1898.

Hays, H. R. *The Dangerous Sex: The Myth of Feminine Evil.* New York: G. P. Putnam's Sons, 1964.

History of Women's Suffrage. Edited by Susan B. Anthony, Elizabeth Cady Stanton, Matilda Joclyn Gage, and Ida Husted Harper, 6 vol. Rochester, New York: 1881, 1886, 1902, 1922.

Aileen S. Kraditor, ed. *Up From the Pedestal.* Chicago: Quadrangle Books, 1968.

Lessing, Doris. *The Golden Notebook.* New York: McGraw-Hill, 1962.

Mill, John Stuart, "The Subjection of Women," *Three Essays.* London: Oxford University Press, 1912.

Millett, Kate. *Sexual Politics.* Garden City, New York: Doubleday & Company, 1970.

Millett, Kate. *Token Learning: A Study of Women's Higher Education in America.* New York: National Organization for Women, 1968.

O'Neill, William L. *Everyone Was Brave: The Rise and Fall of Feminism in America.* Chicago: Quadrangle Books, 1969.

Partinier, Francoise. *An Open Letter to Men.* 1968.

Sampson, R. V. *The Psychology of Power.* New York: Pantheon Books, 1966.

Seidenberg, Robert. *Marriage in Life and Literature.* New York: Philosophical Library, 1970.

Stendahl, Krister. *The Bible and the Role of Women: A Case Study of Hermeneutics.* Philadelphia: Fortress Press, 1966.

U.S. Dept. of Labor. *Handbook of Women Workers,* 1965.

Wollstonecraft, Mary. *A Vindication of the Rights of Women,* 1792.

F-TP

DeCrow, Ka

THE YOUNG

Pegasus, 1

200 pages